The Wonderful Circles of Oz

With the world's economies impacted by coronavirus, billions are feeling social, environmental, and economic injustices. The call for a new, more just, more distributive economic story and system is louder and more urgent than ever. *The Wonderful Circles of Oz* provides both the framework and solutions for navigating towards an effective circular economy – the gateway to an abundant, autonomous, and democratic future.

Widely regarded as one of the world's most engaging circular economy thought leaders, Ken Webster, together with creative writer, Alex Duff, use a storytelling approach based on *The Wonderful Wizard of Oz* to offer a new, accessible, and compelling narrative about the future direction of our economy.

'The harder you work, the more you'll improve your lot.' That's the simple story we've been sold over the last 40 years to justify how today's economy works. Yet extreme inequality, the devastation of our natural world, and the erosion of our communities tell us this economic story resembles a work of fiction and the way our extractive economy operates is not fit for purpose. Still a restoration narrative, a satisfying story about our future and how we'll get there, is slow to emerge. Using allegory, commentary, and reflection, this book helps speed the shift from an extractive economy of materials, energy, and finance to one based on an effective circular economy, which builds wealth as a stock of solutions accessible to all.

The Wonderful Circles of Oz goes beyond tired debates (capital vs labour and market vs state) and blends fiction and non to effectively communicate the need for macro-economic system redesign. Exploring complex change and containing echoes of modern monetary theory, this book is a must for business professionals, students, and anyone with an interest in the circular economy.

Ken Webster is a highly regarded circular economy thought leader. He is credited with setting the intellectual direction for what would become the influential Ellen MacArthur Foundation, where he was Head of Innovation from 2010 to 2018. Dame Ellen (in her autobiography) and others credit Ken with reframing the circular economy concept and enabling the traction it has achieved today. He is a Visiting Fellow at Cranfield University. Ken is a regular contributor and speaker at conferences and seminars around the world and is a Fellow of the Royal Society of Arts.

Alex Duff is an accomplished communicator who helps international leaders creatively turn the complex into compelling. Be they written or spoken, the stories, scripts, and soundbites she's sculpted over the years have been seen and heard on an international stage. She is particularly interested in how fiction can help make abstract topics more accessible so important issues become mainstream.

"This book is a breath-taking journey into intellectual allegories and metaphors of a powerful story... In an era of increasing inequalities, social anxieties and neo-materialism, we need more than ever a story to feed our imagination, a journey to discover sustainable futures, where ideas are the key currency."

Stefano Pascucci, *Professor in Sustainability and Circular Economy, & Head of Sustainable Futures, University of Exeter Business School*

"In these days of a dominance of audio-visual information, the skill of storytelling is one of the keys to get listeners' and readers' attention. By spinning "the golden thread of 'digitally connected systems' to transform our economy" in this book, Ken and Alex prove they are masters in this domain."

Walter Stahel, *Visiting Professor, University of Surrey, & Full Member of the Club of Rome*

"Just as *The Wizard of Oz* was an allegory critiquing the Gold Standard, *The Wonderful Circles of Oz* allegorically introduces us to the actual ways in which money is created, and how they might be harnessed to enable us to create a sustainable economy."

Steve Keen, *Honorary Professor, UCL, & Distinguished Research Fellow, Institute for Strategy, Resilience and Security*

"There is an ongoing debate on resource efficiency in most regions of the world, notably in Europe. Moving from a linear to a circular production model is a primary objective. But to do that the economic policy framework – if not the economic model itself – has to be changed. The incentives structure of today is flawed and for circularity to happen the policy frameworks have to be re-thought. *The Wonderful Circles of Oz* presents a most appealing new narrative which covers the economy as a whole – income distribution, taxation, the right of property owners, debt issues, production and consumption systems, financial system, the digital society and its pros and cons... All in all a very compelling narrative and much needed as inspiration for people around the world who look for solutions to the sustainability dilemma(s)."

Anders Wijkman, *Honorary President, Club of Rome*

The Wonderful Circles of Oz

A Circular Economy Story

Ken Webster and Alex Duff

LONDON AND NEW YORK

Cover image: Olga Domashova
Illustrations: Olga Domashova

First published 2023
by Routledge
4 Park Square, Milton Park, Abingdon, Oxon OX14 4RN

and by Routledge
605 Third Avenue, New York, NY 10158

Routledge is an imprint of the Taylor & Francis Group, an informa business

British Library Cataloguing-in-Publication Data
A catalogue record for this book is available from the British Library

Library of Congress Cataloging-in-Publication Data
Names: Webster, Ken, 1955- author. | Duff, Alex, 1971- author.
Title: The wonderful circles of Oz : a circular economy story / Ken Webster and Alex Duff.
Description: Abingdon, Oxon ; New York, NY : Routledge, 2022. | Includes bibliographical references.
Identifiers: LCCN 2022002622 (print) | LCCN 2022002623 (ebook) | ISBN 9781032109077 (hardback) | ISBN 9781032109107 (paperback) | ISBN 9781003217657 (ebook)
Subjects: LCSH: Sustainable development. | Waste minimization—Economic aspects. | Recycling (Waste, etc.)—Economic aspects. | Environmental economics. | Economics.
Classification: LCC HC79.E5 W438 2022 (print) | LCC HC79.E5 (ebook) | DDC 338.9/27—dc23/eng/20220126
LC record available at https://lccn.loc.gov/2022002622
LC ebook record available at https://lccn.loc.gov/2022002623

ISBN: 978-1-032-10907-7 (hbk)
ISBN: 978-1-032-10910-7 (pbk)
ISBN: 978-1-003-21765-7 (ebk)

DOI: 10.4324/9781003217657

Typeset in Georgia
by codeMantra

Contents

About the authors

Ken Webster and Alex Duff

Ken Webster is a thought leader in the circular economy. He is credited with setting the intellectual direction for what would become the influential Ellen MacArthur Foundation, where he worked as Head of Innovation from 2010 to 2018. After a two-year spell at Exeter University, Ken is now Director of the academically orientated International Society for Circular Economy (IS4CE). He is a Visiting Fellow at Cranfield University, as well as a regular contributor and sought-after speaker at conferences and seminars around the world. Ken is the author of two previous books on this subject – *The Circular Economy: A Wealth of Flows* (2nd edition 2017) and *Sense and Sustainability: Educating for a Circular Economy*, with Craig Johnson (2009). Most recently, Ken has accepted an invitation to join the 21st Century Transformational Economics Commission, part of the Earth4All initiative from the Club of Rome, the Potsdam Institute for Climate Impact Research and partners.

@CircularEconKen

Alex Duff is an accomplished communicator who helps international leaders creatively turn the complex into compelling. Be they written or spoken, the stories, scripts, and soundbites she's sculpted over the years have been seen and heard on an international stage. She is particularly interested in how fiction can help make abstract topics more accessible so important issues become mainstream. It was Ken who sparked Alex's interest in the Circular Economy. The pair met near-on a decade ago, as he embarked on his mission to help frame and establish The Ellen MacArthur Foundation. His innovative thinking (and patience) continues to inspire her and is what led to their collaboration for this book. Alex is the founder of 'not A Duff word'.

@notADuffword

Acknowledgements

With special thanks to Mark Blyth, Steve Keen, Walter R. Stahel, Anders Wijkman, and Alexa Culver for their wise counsel, which (among many things) led to the inclusion of the book's third part.

Thanks especially to the talented Olga Domashova who beautifully illustrated this book and was a pleasure to work with.

To Christina Templeton, Caroline Walker, and Dr Paul Rogers – thank you for your keen eyes that helped prepare the manuscript in its final stages.

With particular thanks to Craig Johnson for allowing us to draw on the Imaginary and the 1.2.4/4 framework in the book Craig and Ken are co-authoring on food systems *ABC&D How to create a regenerative circular economy for all*, published by TerraPreta.

And last but by no means least, thanks to Rebecca Marsh for immediately 'getting' our vision for the book and to the Routledge team for enabling us to make that vision a reality.

Welcome from the authors

This book is based on rewriting the allegory which reputedly underpinned L Frank Baum's book *The Wonderful Wizard of Oz*, published in 1900.

Hugh Rockoff, a distinguished Professor of monetary history at Rutgers, is one of several writers who claimed Baum was writing about his times and the unfair and debilitating consequences of running the US economy based on a gold standard – the commodity-base that controlled the stock of money (Rockoff, 1990).

- Oz = ounce (of gold),
- The yellow brick road = alluding to gold,
- Dorothy's silver slippers = silver bullion – the additional money-base opponents of the gold standard demanded. (Dorothy's slippers in Baum's book are silver, they were changed for visual effect in 1939 for the movie).

And it goes on, with Baum drawing on the rural workforce, represented by the Scarecrow, and industrial workers, represented by the Tin Woodman. But seemingly these parallels – the text is littered with them – have run into the darkness of the unconscious.

Even though Baum never claimed, or even hinted, that this side to his original *The Wonderful Wizard of Oz* was there, both the story and the claims of allegory and metaphor endure.

Baum's time, the 1890s, was an era of extreme inequality and populist resentment. Writers like Mark Twain call this period

DOI: 10.4324/9781003217657-1

the 'Gilded Age', referring to its superficial splendours and its deep poverty. The 'Progressive Era' followed with a different kind of narrative – a swing of the pendulum in the other direction. In some ways, we are in a new 'Gilded Age'. What dominates the 21st century, our age of digital finance, asset inflation, and private debt, are its scions of inequality, stagnant wages, and precariousness. While today's 'Gilded Age' has evolved beyond commodity money (based on those physical goods that hold intrinsic value) to the immaterial, how we build wealth, and who benefits has not evolved and begs for a systemic fix.

In our imagination, ordinary characters are on a bewildering journey to try and reach the Emerald City and find a better understanding. Surely, some Wizard can make it all come right, to help find a way home? Except that what is behind the screen concealing the Wizard might again be much less than it deserves to be.

Our hope is that using allegory can again reveal and preserve ideas relevant to our own times, our new Gilded Age. And, when we are ready, we can reinvent or coalesce around a new Progressive Era.

There is power in metaphor. We ask: What is this experience or idea *like*? We know from cognitive science that almost all our abstract thought is deeply metaphorical. In times of transformation, there is a need to contrast the falling away of the metaphors used in the past with something new. In allegory, where the narrative is the vehicle rather than an image, this process unfolds on a few levels – the obvious and the symbolic, and through this into deeper reflections on the human condition. In search of a different worldview, of seeing where we are now through different eyes, we can take a journey outward and back to ourselves. As T.S. Eliot (1943/2001) wrote in *Little Gidding*: "We shall not cease from exploration, and the end of all our exploring will be to arrive where we started and know the place for the first time." In the contemporary world, it might be possible to find the right images to convey something about what has been changing the way we perceive the past, present, and future.

We are no longer in a world of crude mechanisms and sheet metal, where images of clockworks, bureaucratic hierarchies, demarcated jobs, and the factory whistle are all part of an industrial society. It is digitally networked, fluid connections and interactions that prevail – data flows as much as physical flows. These networks and flows are complex not just complicated. Increasingly, writers like architect William McDonough take insights from living systems or use the lens of biological metabolism as a springboard rather than the physics of machines (McDonough, 2021). This has been underway for decades, but change is slow.

Imagine then, a forest and beneath it an expanding, frequently self-learning collection of networks as the strands of mycelium (the vegetative part of a fungus), undoing and reordering all it touches. In an exact parallel to the internet, it connects beneath the forest floor to provide minerals to the trees in return for sugars. A kind of 'wood-wide-web' (Wohlleben, 2016). Put more simply, digital might be a golden thread, that over time becomes woven into the fabric of our times, just as mycelium is in healthy soils. The dying dominance of the old machines and materials order gives way to digitally connected systems. These started just after the Second World War with the first computers and continue today with our worldwide access to knowledge and each other.

Our new resource is digital information. It is not just connective but *creative*. The more we have, the more possibilities we have. Information reshapes the physical relationships of production, consumption, and exchange – as well as our knowledge space.

If digital resources and tools do not end up primarily as a means of surveillance, population control, or new extractive monopolies, digital can bring the coming Age more autonomy, freedom, and choice about collaboration and association. This is something of a subtext in our *Wonderful Circles of Oz* narrative and its economic framework, developed in our accompanying companion essay, The Imaginary.

We see there being three critical strands to the golden thread of 'digitally connected systems' for transforming our economy.

First, it offers the potential for cheaper tools as well as competitive and collaborative, low-cost social production. It is possible to competitively move to a smaller scale production and consumption model (regional or local), and directly connect with customers cutting out the traditional intermediary from virtual transactions.

Second, digital enables true cost transparency. Materials markers and Artificial Intelligence (AI) enable the monitoring and tracking of products, components, and materials. We can now identify the real costs and extended responsibilities of production and raise fees or charges accordingly. This helps shape markets away from polluting activities and exploitative relationships as their full costs are factored in. We can then fully value renewables, including people, for their positive contribution, so taxation shifts from wages and consumption, towards non-renewables and waste.

Data resources, contributed to by everyone, are a dividend source as much as traditional land, mineral, and energy resources. A person's data is their property. As early as the 1960s, economist Kenneth Boulding suggested: 'An economy is knowledge, energy and materials, with the greatest being knowledge' (Boulding, 1966). Little wonder our digital resources and the knowledge they bring are termed 'the new oil'.

Third, in a changed world, where traditional work and wages are no longer our central axis (climate disruption, inequality, and alienation are), digital, through AI and the automation of all repetitive tasks, has the potential to both increase productivity and retire this kind of work from humans.

From a distribution angle, this is not only about goods and services. A digital infrastructure can easily identify and distribute a basic dividend through digital accounts held at a central bank. A basic dividend that becomes a reality through, among other things, a shift in taxes or fees payable from a myriad of sources – a 'carbon dividend' (Citizen's Climate Lobby, 2021) and other polluting activities that damage our environment, or a share of the 'common-wealth' which has been enclosed and its benefits privately captured. Proposals for a digital dividend are an example (DDP, 2021; FTI, 2021).

Everyone, then, gets a dividend, a share of this income raised, to recognise their share in wealth creation or to enable and reward low impact living or to acknowledge that the infrastructure we all enjoy is part of our endowment. Damping down on the earnings from non-renewables (including non-productive existing assets) brings a productive economy back to the fore.

This is part of an ancient, and seemingly endless, tussle over which is more important – the rights of property to charge for or deny access (enclosure), or the rights of people to meet their own needs from what is common to all. This was the essence of the debate between feudal and mercantile, and in democratic states, between unearned income (rent seeking) and industry (the power to extract wealth versus the need to create wealth and circulate it). It may also be at the heart of our current political malaise if capitalism no longer gets its moral authority from democracy.

To unpack this a little further, it was okay in the industrial era to make profits, interest, and rents because the social contract, framed by democratic overview, was that there were mutual benefits to some of our common inheritance being enclosed for exploitation. But, in our world of seemingly growing inequality, the abandonment of mutuality is a threat to the social contract. What end does democracy serve if it only serves the enclosers and rentiers? If George Cooper is right that essentially 'capitalism accumulates and democracy distributes', it is indeed all about enabling circulation (Cooper, 2014).

In the struggle between extracting rents (unearned income) versus wealth creation and circulation, the UK economist and author Jon Kay (2009) also indicates: 'Almost all the strength of modern market economies is based on directing entrepreneurial activity from rent seeking into wealth creation.'

This is where strength lies – in the productive economy and wealth creation, at all scales.

Our current extractive, linear economy has created scarcity amid plenty, enormous (often toxic) wastes, and substantial unearned incomes. It can teach us about the dangers of the control over access to the new digital tools and resources, falling into relatively few hands.

Digital creates the opportunity for so many to live the lives they choose – lives built on the freedom given by having a basic dividend that removes need. We can all be citizens – willing participants with the time and space to do and enjoy the human pursuits we most value.

The Wonderful Circles of Oz is a journey into some of these ideas and relationships as part of the discussion around the social contract of the future. It strives to contextualise and bring into sharp relief some of the choices before us. It's space to think through perhaps. Like Baum's original story, it's enjoyable just as it is, a story with a moral and a girl... who sells her dog.

References

Boulding, K. E. (1966). The Economics of the Coming Spaceship Earth. In H. Jarrett (Ed.). *Environmental Quality in a Growing Economy*, pp. 3–14. Baltimore, MD: Resources for the Future/Johns Hopkins University Press. [online]. Available at http://arachnid.biosci.utexas.edu/courses/THOC/Readings/Boulding_SpaceshipEarth.pdf [Last accessed 09 May 2021].

Citizen's Climate Lobby. (2021). The Basics of Carbon Fee and Dividend. [online]. Available at https://citizensclimatelobby.org/basics-carbon-fee-dividend/ [Last accessed 09 May 2021].

Cooper, G. (2014). Economics Is a Broken Science: Dr George Cooper on His New Book Money, Blood and Revolution. *World Finance Videos* [online]. Available at https://www.youtube.com/watch?v=P7XGSf-dYyC8 [Last accessed 09 May 2021].

DDP. (2021). *Take Control of Your Data*. Los Angeles: Data Dividend Project. [online]. Available at https://www.datadividendproject.com/ [Last accessed 09 May 2021].

Eliot, T. S. (1943/2001). Little Gidding. In *Four quartets*. London: Faber & Faber.

FTI. (2021). Digital Dividends to Fund Basic Universal Income Plans. *The Future Today Institute*. [online]. Available at https://futuretodayinstitute.com/trend/digital-dividends-to-fund-universal-basic-income-plans/ [Last accessed 09 May 2021].

Kay, J. (2009, June 02) The Rationale of the Market Economy: A European Perspective. [online]. Available at https://www.johnkay.com/2009/06/02/the-rationale-of-the-market-economy-a-european-perspective/ [Last accessed 09 May 2021].

McDonough, W. (2021). Cradle to Cradle. [online]. Available at https://mcdonough.com/cradle-to-cradle/ [Last accessed 09 May 2021].

Rockoff, H. (1990). The "Wizard of Oz" as a Monetary Allegory. *Journal of Political Economy, 98*(4), 739–760. Available at https://courses.cit.cornell.edu/econ1120jpw/readme/wizard%20of%20oz.pdf Last accessed 09 May 2021].

Wohlleben, P. (2016). *The Hidden Life of Trees: What They Feel, How They Communicate*. Vancouver: Greystone Books. Cited in R. Grant (2018). Do Trees Talk to Each Other? *Smithsonian Magazine*, March 2018. [online]. Available at https://www.smithsonianmag.com/science-nature/the-whispering-trees-180968084/ [Last accessed 09 May 2021].

Part one

A fictional world. Rewriting the allegory

1 Weathering extremities

The dairy farm where Dorie lived with her Aunt E was in dire trouble. They'd taken more cows, more machinery, more debt – they could make more milk but, no matter how hard they tried, they just couldn't seem to make more money.

Caving into her aunt's constant pestering, Dorie had begrudgingly taken a supermarket job where she scanned and sold milk for less than it cost her and Aunt E to produce it. In Dorie's mind, the job was a waste of time. The store, on the outskirts of Exeter City, was inconvenient to reach from their semi-rural farm, with shifts ill-timed and sporadic. Dorie was convinced helping Aunt E on their farm would be a much better use of her time.

The infrequent bus service had dropped Dorie on the main road. She walked back towards home along the seemingly never-ending dirt track, surrounded by fields of endless monocultures. It hadn't rained in over a month and the heat was oppressive – as was the stench that seeped from their troubled farm. Her arms ached from carrying bags crammed with food shopping. As she squinted against the sun towards their decaying farmhouse, Dorie saw a fat black Range Rover coming from it. It gained speed showering her in a cloud of dust as it passed.

"Arse," Dorie half spat, half coughed after it, her open mouth filled with dirt. She was still blinking dust from her dry eyes when she reached the courtyard to be greeted by Toto. The faded black dog was too old now to leap and dance around, as he once had, but he was always delighted to see her, and his tail still

DOI: 10.4324/9781003217657-3

wagged excitedly whenever she returned. His unconditional and joyous display of love had never waned, and it made her smile.

Her smile faded though as she stepped into the gloomy kitchen. Even with the windows and doors open, the house always seemed starved of light. Everything looked as neat as always, in its clumsily arranged, piled-high kind of way – but Dorie had known immediately something was wrong. The trouble was Aunt E, in her favourite fading pink day dress, was slouching at the wonky rustic table, her back to the door. Her elbows rested on the table, her dry, ageing hands holding up her head of wispy, greying hair. And *this* was the problem. Aunt E was seemingly doing absolutely nothing. Dorie knew no matter how bad things were or how frequent her aunt's complaints of constant exhaustion, Aunt E never did nothing.

Dorie plonked two heavy bags of shopping on the table and some of their contents spewed out.

"Got us some bargains," Dorie said to her aunt through a forced smile. She was trying, unsuccessfully, to break her aunt from stillness and from another of her increasingly frequent dark moods. If Aunt E heard her niece she didn't react, her gaze unwavering. Unsure how best to proceed, Dorie begun unpacking the shopping. But her aunt's silence was eerie. She was quick to temper, not a strong, silent type. So, after only a few minutes, Dorie placed a hand on her aunt's shoulder.

"Aunt E, you okay?" she said softly, gently shaking her as if to wake her from sleep.

"We've lost it," she almost whispered. "They're going to take the farm Dorie."

***

There was nothing to be heard except the occasional slurp of tea that Dorie and Aunt E drank from chipped mugs as they sat at the table opposite each other. Dorie thought but didn't say: 'Why would anyone want to take a farm that couldn't make money?' What did that mean for them?' Somehow, she didn't think now was the time for such questions. But Dorie couldn't think of anything comforting to say, so the pair continued slowly sipping their steaming, sweet tea in silence.

A strong gust of wind blew through the farmhouse, slamming shut the rotting wooden-framed kitchen window. The noise made Aunt E jump and drop her mug. It bounced off the table and shattered against the flagstone floor. Startled by the commotion, Toto leapt from where he had been snoozing under the table and ran into the courtyard. Dorie hurried to the window and secured the latch, relieved to see the pane still intact. She peered out of it and saw what had become a threatening sky.

"Wow, what's going on?" Dorie said aloud but mainly to herself. "That wind's really picked up."

She turned the radio on to hear the newsreader say: 'After the driest year on record and following weeks of relentless heat, a tornado is heading through the county. On the leading edge of a cold front, it's expected to bring much needed rain, although this will possibly be torrential in places. The Government's advice is to get indoors and seek shelter in the lowest level of your home. Keep away from all windows. And keep your pets tied up or crated.'

"Toto," Dorie yelled. She ran into the courtyard to find the little dog frightened and disorientated, howling and jumping around. As she scooped Toto into her arms the tornado's circular and powerful force hit the farm. A gust of wind knocked Dorie off her feet and she fell to the ground. Everything around her dissolved into chaos. Then there was nothing.

2 From poor to paws

Dorie wakes to find Toto licking her face.

"Yuck," she says pushing him away and brushing the drool from her cheek with the back of her hand. Sitting herself upright, she exclaims: "Ow."

"Heavy night was it?" says a bemused voice behind her.

Startled, Dorie clambers to her feet. "No," she says, "I was swept up in a tornado, fell from the sky and hit my head."

"Ah ha," says a plain greying lady in a royal blue trouser suit, clearly disbelieving her.

"Where am I?" asks Dorie looking around, slightly startled by how bright, clean, and green everything seems.

"You're in Oz," replies the grey lady. "Where's home?"

"Exeter, it's in Devon, do you know it?" Dorie asks.

"No, I'm afraid I've never heard of it, but Oz is an amazing place, you'll love it here. If you hang around, you might find you'd prefer to stay."

"I can't possibly stay. I've got to get home. Aunt E just had some dreadful news and I really need to get back to her."

"Well, that's a shame. I'm the Mayor – the *People's* Mayor." She labours the word *people's* and pauses, like she's expecting a reaction from Dorie – perhaps waiting for her to connect with what she's just said and all it implies. When the only reaction she gets is one of puzzlement, she continues: "Then I'm afraid I can't help you. If it's that important to you, you'll have to go to the Emerald City and seek out the Great Wizard to help you get home."

DOI: 10.4324/9781003217657-4

"The Great Wizard? An Emerald City?" Dorie's head is still fuzzy but she's getting a sense of déjà vu. "Okay," Dorie continues, "how do I get there?"

"Well, that depends," replies the grey lady. "How much money have you got?"

Dorie looks down; she's wearing leggings and a baggy t-shirt. It's her attempt at hiding her growing waistline, which she knows is a result of all the cheap, unhealthy, food she and Aunt E have lived on lately. She'd picked the outfit up at the supermarket – it had been under a fiver, but there are no pockets. "Err, none," says Dorie.

"That means you'll have to walk. It's quite a distance, it will take you a few days."

Dorie gets a spark of recognition. "Let me guess, you are going to give me a pair of silver slippers and set me on the right path?" She pauses momentarily. "No not a path, a road paved with yellow bricks?"

The grey lady laughs. "You really did hit your head hard," she says. "Why would I do that? Your shoes look perfectly fine to me. You're in Oz – we have autonomy here and," sliding into typical politician mode, she finishes her sentence with, "you can mostly choose your own path in life and certainly into the Emerald City." Dorie's unsure how she's supposed to respond to that, but it doesn't matter because the grey lady keeps on talking. "It's a long walk though and while our land is plentiful, you'll need to buy some supplies before you set off."

"But I have no money," says Dorie.

The grey lady looks down at the scruffy, greying dog laying across Dorie's feet, then opens her big, black handbag and pulls out her purse. "We don't see many of that breed," she says. "I've got £50.00 here, I'll give you that for him."

"Sell Toto?" Dorie says aghast. "I couldn't do that."

"Well, it doesn't look like you've got anything else to bargain with."

"Can't you just lend me some money?" says Dorie earnestly. "I'll pay you back when I get home."

"Look Dorie. I love my job and my land. I'm paid a fair wage for a fair day's work but I'm not rich and I can't afford to be dishing out money to every stranger that happens to end up here. If it makes your decision any easier, the dog will only hold you up anyway. You'll be travelling through different lands to get to the Emerald City and he'll need a pet passport – I'm guessing you don't have one?"

Dorie shakes her head. She looks down to the little mutt at her feet. She scoops him up in her arms, rubs his head and says: "Be good boyo. Aunt E and I are broke, we're losing the farm, you'll have happier last years here". Then, she hands him over to the grey lady, who puts him in her handbag – his little greying head poking out of the top. Dorie takes the money and, as she hasn't any pockets, tucks the notes into her bra for safe keeping. "I'd better get going before I change my mind."

"I understand," says the grey lady. "There are a few shops just around the corner where you can get your supplies. Anyone will be able to point you in the right direction to the Emerald City." Then, without another word, the grey lady turns on her low, fat, black heel and walks away. A small, pathetic whimpering comes from within her handbag, which swings by her side as she carries Toto away.

3 From straw for brains to wise owls

Dorie doesn't feel as bad as you might think, despite finding herself in an unknown place, selling Toto, and having a long walk ahead. The countryside is beautiful, varied, and plentiful. There are enormous trees bearing fruit, colourful plants abuzz with wildlife and lush green hedgerows housing songful birds.

Wearing her comfiest old trainers, and with a new backpack holding her supplies, Dorie feels good. After walking for some hours, she needs to rest. She settles on a grassy green bank alongside a golden cornfield with blood red poppies hugging its perimeter. The field, set against a perfect blue sky, is complete with its own scarecrow. It's rather odd looking, dressed in a weathered, zip-down, hooded owl onesie. Bored with the silence of having travelled alone for so long she says: "Hello Mr Scarecrow, fancy joining me for some lunch?" before looking down to unzip her backpack.

"Don't mind if I do," replies the scarecrow, smiling from under his orange-beaked hood.

Alarmed, Dorie asks: "Did you speak?"

"Yes, I did," replies the scarecrow jumping down from his post. "You did invite me to remember?"

"Err, of course," says Dorie still unsure what to make of this. She's not scared. He seems so friendly and she's sure she's heard about a talking scarecrow somewhere before but for the life of her she can't seem to recall where. She offers him half a triangle of sandwich, which he takes beaming from ear to ear.

DOI: 10.4324/9781003217657-5

D.O.

"You look too happy to scare off crows," says Dorie by way of breaking the ice.

"I'm not here to scare off crows," says the scarecrow.

"Oh?" says Dorie puzzled.

"No, we have companion planting and other farming methods to keep natural pests away now. See how in this field we are growing corn, beans, and squash altogether? They each help the other in some way to reach their full potential and that helps maximise our harvest."

"Oh," is the only response Dorie can muster – not sure if she is more surprised by the scarecrow's sales pitch or apparent horticultural knowledge. "But if that works, then why are you here?"

"I'm here to keep the unnatural pests away," says the scarecrow, his voice quietening to a whisper, "the land vultures". Then, as if catching himself, he leans away from Dorie and adds suspiciously: "You're not one, are you?"

"No," says Dorie, slightly offended but with great certainty. "I'm just a lost girl. I'm only passing through on my way to the Emerald City. You see I'm going to find the Great Wizard to ask him if he can help get me home."

The scarecrow frowns, pausing a beat as though debating whether he should say something. He settles on: "Oh, that's a shame. If I'm honest I was secretly hoping you were one. You see the Wizard made some adjustments and introduced a land value fee in Oz a few years ago. Since then, I've rarely seen anything resembling a land vulture and it can get a little boring out here all day on my own. Do you want to see me in scary mode?"

"Err no, probably not, says Dorie. Then, noticing his disappointment, she hurriedly adds: "It's just, like I already said, you seem more smart than scary." The scarecrow warms again at that. "I'm afraid I don't really know what a land vulture is or anything about land value fees so I'm not sure I can help you," says Dorie.

"People make it sound difficult but it's not really," says the scarecrow. "You see, it used to be that vultures would swoop in and eat up all the land. Once they got their claws into it, you couldn't get them out again. It's bad enough, having uninvited visitors but then they'd outstay their welcome, start bossing everyone around, before going onto charge us to stay here, keeping all the surplus for themselves. It was going on all through Oz, until the Wizard decided enough was enough. The Wizard said that because there's only a limited supply of land, something that's valuable and belongs to everyone, those fortunate enough to get some to themselves, should pay an annual fee all the time they have it. The fee is for them getting private benefit from what's really a valuable and shared asset. It's a kind of compensation for them making that piece of land unavailable as a shared resource – the fee they pay instead benefits everybody. Anyway, since it came in, there's been fewer vultures and things have seemed much better."

"It seems fair that something that belongs to everyone, benefits everyone," says Dorie, "but if the vultures have gone, why do you stay doing this job?"

"Because Oz is a democracy, and we have to protect it. That means staying alert - so that's what I'm doing. Just keeping my eye on things here to be sure those vultures don't return."

Dorie's unsure how to reply to that. From the way he speaks she can't help but wonder if he's a friend of the Mayor. She's heard of citizens being active in community matters back home but she can't think of any of her friends who seem as committed to the cause as this scarecrow. He's even dressed himself as an owl to help scare away any vultures that might happen to fly over. She can't decide if it's commendable or committable, which means it's probably safer to change the subject.

"I'm from a farm back home," Dorie tells the scarecrow. "We only have cows on it though."

"Just cows?" says the scarecrow surprised. "We have a real mix of stuff here – cows, chickens, crops. You must be a great cow farmer to be able to make a living from just the one thing."

Dorie's heart sinks at his comment. "Well actually things haven't been going so well for us lately. I'd be really interested in seeing what you do here. Do you think you'd be able to take a break from your field to show me around?"

"I'd love to," says the scarecrow proudly. "What are we waiting for?" He jumps softly onto his feet.

***

By the time they've finished touring the farm, Dorie's head is spinning. She's never seen anything like it.

"Of course, we don't always get it right," the scarecrow is telling her. "These more mixed and regenerative methods keep us all on our toes, well, for those of us who have toes," he half laughs, shaking his straw leg at her. "You can often be wrong-footed by nature because it's always evolving. Last year the weather was particularly cool, and seed corn maggots invaded my field - we lost the lot. It cost us all dearly but me particularly – I literally got eaten alive and needed re-stuffing. It was awful but our farming methods mean we're never dependent on any one income stream. Crucially, they keep our soil strong. So, when things go wrong, we have a solid base from which to work and can just adapt what we do and try something else."

They are back at the edge of the scarecrow's field now. "Thanks so much for the tour," Dorie says.

"My pleasure," says the scarecrow beaming proudly again at her. "It has cheered up my day but," he continues, nodding towards his field with the breath-taking view, "I guess I really ought to be getting back to my post."

Dorie senses his hesitation. "Look, I'm going to find the Great Wizard to ask him to get me home," she says. "You could come with me. Perhaps you could ask him about those land vultures you are watching for – what they look like and whether he thinks any will be coming back any time soon."

"Oh no, I couldn't do that," says the scarecrow. "What if they were to return while I was gone? No, it's kind of you to offer, but I think I'll stay put. My days can be a little boring, but I need to hold my post for a while longer yet - just to be sure. Plus, I love life here on the farm."

Dorie can see why. Yet, she senses the story she's vaguely starting to recollect isn't supposed to go this way. She's sure the scarecrow is meant to join her on her journey to the Emerald City. Still, she guesses, his decision is understandable. While he's confused about his purpose, he seems happy and life on the farm is good enough for him.

Dorie bids the scarecrow farewell and continues her journey alone. A gentle mizzle falls, cooling Dorie's face and filling her nostrils with the most wonderful earthy smell. 'It even smells better here than home,' she muses. As she reaches a turn in the road, she glances back to see the scarecrow has returned to his post and is scanning the horizon for enemies that will never come.

4 Heartless

If only AI had EI

DOI: 10.4324/9781003217657-6

Lost in her thoughts, Dorie is enjoying the peacefulness of her surroundings when a groan breaks the silence. Curious, she steps off the path and heads towards a small wood. Standing at its edge, under the shade of an apple tree, she strains to listen. She hears another groan and walks into the wood's darkness until she comes to a clearing. In the middle, she sees what looks like a man, made entirely of tin. Piles of perfectly separated out metal items – which look a lot like computer parts – surround him.

A glimpse of a childhood story comes flooding back to Dorie. The surroundings aren't exactly as she remembers them but she's confident – this is the tin woodman and he's going to need her help.

"Did you groan?" asks Dorie.

The tin woodman spins around and Dorie jumps back, surprised by the sudden movement.

"No, I certainly did not," says the tin woodman. "That's the sound the Next Gen 101s make when I take them apart."

"Okay," says Dorie, unsure how to respond to that. Then, composing herself, Dorie sticks her hand out by way of introduction and says, "I'm guessing you are the tin woodman?"

"I am certainly no such thing," says the tin looking man, seemingly most offended and ignoring her outstretched hand. "I am the Nexus 209 robot with artificial intelligence capabilities." She's just about to introduce herself but it continues on: "I'm the ultimate in terms of artificial intelligence advancement. As you can see," the robot indicates to the piles of metal stacked high around it, "it has taken a while to perfect the tech but there's never been a more powerful and useful version than me, Nexus 209. Everything that came before me is now redundant."

"Oh," says Dorie. "Is that what you are doing? Breaking up the old stuff and dumping it out here in the wood to get rid of it?"

"Get rid of it? Why on earth would I do that? No, while they've surpassed their usefulness as robots, there's still plenty of life left in their parts. We make everything from the outset for disassembly. It means when this happens," the robot points to the piles of old computer parts around it, "we can easily take our stuff apart and reuse the materials for something else. I'm even made that way. Although I'll never suffer this sorry fate thank goodness."

"Why not?" asks Dorie.

"Because," says the robot. "I'm the ultimate upgrade. There's never been a more intelligent version, there never will be, and demand for me and my fellow Nexus 209s has been unprecedented."

Dorie frowns, she knows from her smartphone experiences that this is very unlikely. How can evolution be over she thinks, but she has the good sense to remain quiet. She feels sorry for this robot. She assumes someone has programmed it to genuinely believe it will never become obsolete. She realises the robot is looking expectantly at her. "Err, unprecedented demand," she says, reminding herself of what it was saying. "What's driving that then?"

"Well Dorie," the robot replies, "it's because I'm so helpful to humans."

Dorie is confused, she's sure she didn't tell this thing her name and she's beginning to get a little creeped out. After all, she is travelling alone and is in the middle of nowhere. Distractedly trying to remember if she told it her name or not, she asks: "How is it helpful to humans?"

"In so many ways," says the robot. "Just look at what I'm doing here, dismantling all this redundant stuff. That's such a boring thing for a human to have to do, now they don't need to."

"Yeah, we've automated a lot of mundane factory jobs back home as well," says Dorie.

"Oh, that's just one example. We're using intelligent technologies extensively throughout Oz now. There's a fellow self-learning Nexus like me in the Emerald City, working with doctors. It's nearly twice as likely to correctly diagnose lung cancer than its human equivalent."

"Wow that's life changing," says Dorie. But then she starts to think about it. Self-learning machines that are smarter than people. Great all the time they're doing something good, like saving lives, but she's seen the movies – what's to stop them going beyond their remit if they are already smarter than people?

Dorie decides it might be better to keep that thought to herself as well, so she continues: “Doesn’t everyone here hate you for taking their jobs?”

“Quite the contrary,” the robot explains. “We give back precious time to humans. We exist to give them the freedom to engage in more creative pursuits.”

Dorie frowns again. That sounds unlikely. Surely if artificial intelligence is replacing so many jobs in Oz, people wouldn’t be able to afford to engage in ‘more creative pursuits’? Perhaps, she thinks, this robot is devious. Perhaps it has learnt to lie. Perhaps, she decides, it would be better to get going. And with that she says, “I’m sorry but I really need to get going. I’m off to...”

“...See the Great Wizard in the Emerald City?” the robot cuts in, finishing her sentence.

“How could you know that?” Dorie questions warily.

“Haven’t you been listening to anything I’ve told you Dorie?” the robot responds. “I’m Nexus 209 – the ultimate artificial intelligence – designed to help humans with their every need and move. I, for example, can calculate the probability of someone like you reaching the Emerald City.”

“So, you can take me to the Emerald City then?” Dorie asks, suddenly more hopeful that this entire encounter might lead to something useful.

“No,” says the robot in its cold and matter-of-fact tone. “I told you, Nexus 209 is in great demand and I’m needed here. I’ve calculated there’s a 98.34% chance you’ll make it to the Emerald City unaccompanied. Just keep an eye out for those lions and tiger-headed bears and you should be fine. Your journey just isn’t a priority for me.”

“Oh,” says Dorie again, trying to be neither offended nor alarmed. She’s sure, in the story she remembers, the two of them are supposed to journey onwards together and become firm friends.

“Best I can do is give you directions for the quickest route into the Emerald City and provide your estimated arrival time if you take it,” concludes the robot, which it promptly tells her before turning back to its work to destroy its lineage.

5 Making the lion's share enough to go around

Dorie is thinking about stopping to rest again when ahead she sees a lion. He's in a layby behind a market stall of sorts, displaying bottles of something. Dorie's unsure why but she's not scared, indeed she's expecting the lion to be scared at her approach. She's surprised to hear him roar out: "Come and get your courage cider. All made right here with locally grown organic apples."

"Mm, that sounds delicious," replies Dorie: "How much?"

"Three bottles for £10.00," says the lion.

Given how little money she has this is clearly an extravagance, but after the day she's had Dorie just fancies a cold, refreshing cider. Diving into her bra, she pulls out a note and hands it over. The lion takes it, replacing the note with his oversized paw to shake her hand.

"A pleasure doing business with you. I'm William Jennings Bryan Junior," he says.

"Gosh, that's a big name. I'm Dorie," says Dorie.

"Yes, having to live in the shadow of my grandfather can be difficult but I'm trying to find my own path," replies the lion.

Dorie has no idea what he's talking about. She's quite sure she's never heard of his grandfather – she'd simply meant it was rather a long name for a lion. Instead, she says: "And your own path is..." She trails off, raising the inflection in her voice to make it sound like a question.

"... Community-based entrepreneur," the lion says finishing her sentence. "A few years ago, I was a dying breed. Then, the

DOI: 10.4324/9781003217657-7

Apple Cider
D.O.

Great Wizard introduced a basic dividend in Oz – now instead of being next on the extinction list local ventures like mine have been thrown a lifeline."

Having drunk half the bottle of cider, Dorie is beginning to feel more confident about admitting her lack of knowledge. "A basic dividend? Never heard of it. We don't have that where I live and I'm from a family farm, so I guess I'm considered a dying breed. What is it? Try not to make it too complicated though – this stuff is going straight to my head," she says, tapping her finger against the bottle's neck.

"Don't worry, there's nothing complicated about it – you simply get money for being a citizen of Oz. It doesn't matter who you are or how much money you have, everyone gets the same. If you're rich and you don't want it you can give it away but, if you aren't, you can use it for whatever you want."

"Free money? For doing nothing?" questions Dorie disbelievingly.

"Well, you're supposed to do *something* productive with it. You invest it in yourself to create a return for you over time. It provides a foundation on which to do something courageous. For me, that was making a real go at this brewing and bottling cider business. It's like start-up funding or venture capital, but for individuals."

"Venture capital for the people – that's brilliant," says Dorie, suppressing a small hiccup and tapping her finger against the bottle again, which is now nearly empty.

"It really is," says the lion proudly: "Both the product and the production. I get surplus organic apples from a nearby orchard. I employ local people to help me make it. I sell it locally but while we've been chatting," he pauses and looks down at his smartphone, "I've also sold 15 crates online to go further afield. And look where I'm based – practically in the middle of nowhere."

"What does it matter where you're based?" asks Dorie.

"It matters a lot to this community. I'm creating wealth here and keeping it circulating locally. That's the best ten quid you'll spend today."

"Really?" says Dorie, unsure of what the lion is getting at.

"You've just helped build the wealth of this little community. How can communities be, well communities, if all a business does is take money out from those that live there and divert it to some central point miles away? A community doesn't create itself. It needs time, money, and effort to make it flourish. My business helps keep money recirculating right here."

"So, you're more than a local entrepreneur," says Dorie, "you're creating a localised vortex that sucks in, circulates and spreads community wealth."

"Exactly," says the lion, thrilled that his customer seems to appreciate his valuable contribution and to have grasped the concept's advantages.

"Then, why would you worry about living in the shadow of your grandfather? I can't imagine him being anything other than impressed with your achievements."

"I don't think so," responds the lion, hanging his head in what Dorie thinks resembles shame. "I don't think one of the greatest political visionaries would be proud of my choice of venture."

"Why not?" Dorie asks.

"Because his work about the importance of having enough money flowing in society remains unfinished. You see if there's not enough cash in the system it hampers exchange. That hampers business, which hampers prosperity, and that's not good for anyone."

"Hmm, so you not only carry his name, but feel you also carry a responsibility to finish his work?" says Dorie.

"It feels more like a burden than a responsibility," replies the lion, then adds: "Local businesses keep money circulating locally and working it hard to become a community force for good. But cash certainly seems to be getting harder to come by out here. That's why I've taken my grandfather's work a step further, putting more money into our local economy by introducing these tokens... See?" The lion reaches down to the table and picks up a metallic coin embossed around the outer edge with: 'Courageous community coinage' and a value of '1sPence' stated clearly in the middle. On the flip side is a slogan: "If you want apples you have to shake the tree".

"You introduced your own local currency?" asks Dorie, surprised.

"Well yes, to complement the national one," says the lion. "Just swapping one for the other doesn't add any spending power, which defeats the whole point – so there's extra spending power here. Just as there's room in the market for locally, nationally, or globally produced cider, you can do money on different scales. These coins are actually made from my cider's recycled steel bottle tops."

"And people use them?" Dorie is astonished.

"Of course," says the lion, surprised by her surprise. "I'm a respected figure in this community. My family has long-standing. People here trust me and that extends to these tokens. I mean, don't get me wrong, people aren't just trusting in them because of my family's name – they are backed by my savings – but trust matters because people want to know the tokens are worth something. Once that confidence is there though, what you've created is additional spending power."

"I just don't get it – how?" says Dorie frowning.

"Okay think about it like this. If you'd rocked up here today without any cash, what could you have bought from me?"

"Nothing," says Dorie.

"Exactly. You wouldn't have been able to buy my cider. Which means you'd be thirsty, and I'd be £10 down. That's a tenner I can't now spend myself or invest in bettering my business and neither can the next person I'd have spent that tenner with."

"Yes, I get that bit but how do the tokens help?" says Dorie.

"Yesterday there was no £10.00 and no tokens. I can't control the availability of money governed centrally or its flow, but today there are these tokens – I've created credit. Let's rerun the scenario. What's in your backpack?"

Dorie opens her backpack and says: "Six apples?"

"Excellent! I'm a cider producer, apples are my thing – they'll help my business be more productive. I'll buy those off you in exchange for two tokens."

"Okay," says Dorie. "What do I get for two tokens?"

"One will buy you a bottle of my cider. The other you can spend as you pass through the village. You must spend your tokens here though because nobody beyond this community accepts them. When you exchange them, you set off a chain of activity that otherwise wouldn't have happened here."

"I see. Because I've spent this token with you, you can now also spend it locally and so it goes on," says Dorie.

"Exactly. But you need money in the system to set things in motion and you want to keep it circulating – in this instance, locally. The more these tokens change hands, the more demand they create and the more community good they do. They've certainly helped increase local economic activity here. But therein lies the problem. I just have this constant nagging feeling that were my grandfather still here, he'd be asking why I'd settled for transforming a single community when I could be campaigning to finish his work and transform all of Oz."

"Well, what would you have to do to do that?" Dorie asks him.

"Go into politics," the lion pauses, "and who in their right mind would want to do that? Plus, everyone would unfavourably compare me to my grandfather – I'm not known beyond this community and I'm not a natural public speaker."

"Nobody's born a great public speaker, it takes years of practice. I'm sure if your grandad were here, he'd be the first to tell you that."

"I'm just not that brave," says the lion despondently.

"Look, I don't know much about politics or public speaking but I'm off to see the Great Wizard in the Emerald City. I'm going to ask him to get me home. If you come with me, I'm sure he'll be able to give you some coaching and confidence to help you speak up and scale your ideas."

The lion looks at Dorie in a slightly puzzled way. She thinks he may be about to say something but seems to change his mind. "It's a good plan," he says eventually. "I've often wondered what it would feel like to acquire the type of fame my grandfather had in his time."

"Great, it's settled then, you'll come with me," Dorie says, finally feeling like things are falling into place.

"No, sorry, I just can't. Honestly, I admire the journey you are on to find the Wizard and secure what you want but it just feels like an awful lot of effort, for what might end up being little return for me. My grandfather had a great idea but, ultimately, he died without realising it. I guess I'm doing alright. It may be small scale, but I've evolved his thinking and proved it works. Plus, like you said, I've got an important role as a local entrepreneur helping create, circulate, and spread community wealth. Life here is good. I think I'd rather stick with what I know."

How disappointing, thinks Dorie. Such a magnificent creature, wasting such a massive opportunity. And she can't put her finger on it, but there's something about everything he's said. She's sure, were he more courageous, the connection he's made between a flourishing currency and community would just be the start. Sad as it is though, Bryan the lion has made his decision, so she politely says her goodbyes and continues her journey alone.

6 Locked in the past

Dorie is weary from walking, but she ups her pace as dusk falls. Then, she sees it – what can only be the Emerald City, silhouetted against a burnt red sky. She's relieved but as she approaches her relief wanes. Ahead is a huge, locked titanium steel gate blocking her path into the walled city. She pushes and pulls but the gate doesn't budge. Set into the gate's ironwork is a symbol...

That must be a code she thinks but she can't see a keypad. In a last ditch attempt she tries, "Open Sesame".

"Open Sesame," a masculine voice says mockingly. "Really? We're not in Ali Baba and the forty thieves." A thin looking older man, wearing a crumpled Emerald Green guard's uniform, steps into view.

"I'm the only one who can open the gate," he says producing an oversized steel key. "Listen to this." He pushes the key into

DOI: 10.4324/9781003217657-8

the lock and turns it. The internal mechanism clunks open. "Sounds beautiful doesn't it?"

"Err, yes?" says Dorie, not sure what else to say but slightly underwhelmed by hearing it unlock.

"You won't hear that anywhere else in the Emerald City. And they only keep this one for posterity," says the dishevelled, uniformed man nostalgically.

"Don't tell me, things are so great here you don't have to keep anything locked up?" asks Dorie.

"Don't be daft," he replies. "This is a big city. There's plenty of crime, we still need locks, it's just nobody uses the real thing anymore."

"The real thing?" questions Dorie.

"Yes, a lock and key like this," he says, pointing at the oversized steel key again. "I spent my life as a locksmith. My father and his father before him were locksmiths but all the tech advances put me out of business. Nobody wants a traditional lock and key anymore – it's all automated now."

"Oh, I can imagine that's upsetting," says Dorie empathetically, albeit a little impatiently. She's keen to get into the city, not hear his life story or delusions.

"I took the job to preserve this lock – it's a very important part of our heritage you know. I don't even have to keep the gate locked but I just love that sound and it reminds me of the good old days."

"You don't need to lock the gate?" questions Dorie. "What are you supposed to do here then?"

"I'm the gate greeter. I'm here to give a warm welcome to everyone who arrives at the gateway to the Emerald City," the gate greeter says, parodying the corporate speak of his job description.

Dorie can't help but think if that's his role he isn't particularly good at it. So far, he hasn't smiled, he's mocked her and significantly slowed her journey. "It's a bit ironic you having this job isn't it?" Dorie says instead. "You spent all those years keeping people out and now here you are in a role designed to welcome people in?"

"I never thought about it like that," responds the gate greeter. "I've just made the role my own. I believe it's the perfect example of old- meets new- world."

Dorie raises an eyebrow, but the old man doesn't seem to notice. He just continues on: "After I went out of business, I was lonely at home all day. I took this job to meet people. Then I realised by locking the gate I could have the best of both worlds. Now I welcome people into the Emerald City AND preserve the finest lock in the land. It's actually a very important job."

It sounds to Dorie that he's trying to convince himself, rather than her. She probes a little further: "You didn't fancy a complete change then? You could have done anything couldn't you?"

"There's enough change in this land without me adding to it," snaps the gate greeter. Then, his voice softening, he says: "You know what they say about old dogs and new tricks."

The phrase leads Dorie's mind back to Toto. How could she have left the little mutt to start a new life at his age? He hadn't been able to learn many tricks even as a pup. Dorie suddenly feels sad and tired and is keen to get going but the old gate greeter is still talking at her in his rather depressing tone.

"This may not be the city's best job, but what are my options? I've had plenty of time here to contemplate the future but the longer I think about it, the less sense it makes. Everyone seems to welcome all this change and new technology, but it has been the ruin of me."

Dorie can see he's lost in his thoughts now, so she shifts her weight, and her movement brings the gate greeter back into the moment. "Sorry, where were we?" he says.

"Technology," Dorie replies reluctantly.

"Oh yes. That reminds me, you need to wear this while you are in the Emerald City and return it before you leave." He digs into his inside jacket pocket and, to Dorie's visible surprise, pulls out a smartwatch.

As the gate greeter straps it to her wrist the screen lights up and Dorie's name flashes across it.

"Why do I need this and how does it know who I am?" Dorie asks looking at it suspiciously.

"Well, I haven't a clue *how* it works. I find all this tech stuff completely bewildering but Nexus 209 sent an alert that you were coming and what time you'd likely arrive," says the gate greeter matter-of-factly. "I don't wear one myself but, *apparently*," he stresses the word 'apparently' in a sarcastic way, "this smartwatch helps you get around the city." Dorie isn't convinced but when he explains it's how the Wizard's office will contact her, she reluctantly lowers her arm in acceptance. Meeting the Wizard is, after all, the reason she has travelled so far.

7 Technological wizardry or trickery?

It had all been going so well half an hour ago. Dorie had figured out how to find somewhere to stay on the smartwatch and had been following directions towards it. But now she's sure she's lost, it's dark, and she's tired. 'It's not that smart,' she thinks, turning into a side street. She takes a few paces into the dark, narrow alley, attempting to trick the machine into updating its directions from her new location. She's so focused on the watch that she fails to hear something swooping in behind her. Then, for the second time in a day, Dorie's world goes black.

***

"Miss, miss. Can you hear me?" Dorie blearily opens her eyes to find two medics in emerald green uniforms looming over her.

"What happened?" Dorie asks.

"Sit up slowly. You've taken a blow to the back of the head," says the male medic.

"But I just got here," says Dorie. This was hardly the welcome she'd been expecting. No wonder the scarecrow, robot, and lion hadn't wanted to join her going into the Emerald City.

The other, female, medic smiles at her. "The good news is you're going to be fine," she says.

"What's the bad news?" Dorie asks, knowing bad news always follows someone's first good news offering.

"You've been robbed," says the male medic.

Dorie looks around her. "Oh no. My bag's gone?"

DOI: 10.4324/9781003217657-9

"So's your smartwatch," continues the male medic. "That's most likely what they were after. The bag was just a bonus, taken in case it contained cash. Thieving monkeys."

Dorie groans, her head hurting. "How did you find me?"

"Ironically, through your smartwatch. It not only tracks your location but your health. We knew you were in trouble when your heart rate elevated and then the watch went dark," says the female medic.

"I'm grateful," says Dorie, "but it feels rather creepy that you can just track people like that. Where I'm from that would never be allowed. People would have a fit if they thought the authorities could track their every move."

"Tech companies had been tracking people for years here without anyone really understanding what was going on and without any controls. The Wizard just helped people understand, embraced the technology, and put it to good use. As you've seen it doesn't stop crime, but it certainly helps response times," says the female medic.

"The difficulty is, all that tech in a watch is valuable," says the male medic, "and newly arriving visitors are easy pickings because they have to wear one."

Dorie can't help but feel cynical. 'There's probably a gang hacking the tech and tracking people through it,' she thinks but, not wanting to sound ungrateful, keeps her thoughts to herself.

"Well, I don't know what I'm going to do now," Dorie finally says. "Virtually everything I had was in that bag." She tucks her hand down her top and retrieves the remaining notes from her bra. "I've got thirty quid to my name."

"Look, I'm getting off shift now," says the female medic. "I've got a spare room that I let out sometimes to get extra cash in but it's empty tonight. Come back and stay at mine. Don't worry about the money for now." She outstretches her hand. "My name's Glinda by the way."

***

It's mid-morning by the time Dorie wakes. So exhausted was she last night that she'd barely noticed her surroundings or had the energy for polite conversation, retiring to her room quickly and falling into a deep sleep. Now she pulls open the curtains in her small but comfortable room, she's surprised to find herself in the hub of the Emerald City with a fantastic view. 'I wonder how she affords an apartment like this as a medic,' Dorie thinks. The thought is broken by the amazing smell of bacon wafting through. It entices her out of her room towards the kitchen where she finds Glinda busy cooking.

"Good morning, sleepy head," says Glinda smiling.

"Is it? Still morning?" asks Dorie suppressing a yawn. "I feel like I've been asleep for days."

"Good. Sleep is still one of the best healers," says Glinda without a jot of irony. "How are you feeling?"

Dorie instinctively touches the back of her head. "Tender," she says, "but remarkably good given my day yesterday. Thanks for last night."

Glinda waves away her comment with her hand. "Fancy a BaKind sarnie?" Glinda says by way of response.

"I'm famished, yes please I'd love one. There's nothing like the smell of frying bacon," says Dorie, automatically taking in a deep breath to savour the smell.

"Well, it's not actually bacon."

"Really?" Dorie lifts the corner of the bread suspiciously to examine the contents of the sandwich Glinda has put in front of her.

"Just try it," says Glinda, watching Dorie closely.

"It's delicious," says Dorie taking a bite. "What is it?"

"Believe it or not, it's plant based – full of protein."

"Don't suppose your pig farmers are too happy?" says Dorie between giant mouthfuls.

Glinda laughs. "There weren't any left to upset. Livestock farms had already morphed into industrial-scale factories. Tens of thousands of animals, born, bred and dead under one cramped roof. It was like prison for pigs without parole. Needless-to-say, it wasn't good for them and, as it turns out, it wasn't good for us or the land of Oz either, so the Wizard put a stop to it. Now you're hard pushed to find animal meat sold anywhere in Oz."

Dorie puts her sandwich down in surprise. "The Great Wizard just told people they couldn't eat animal meat anymore and they didn't? There would be uproar where I come from if you told people they couldn't have steak and chips."

"Don't be daft! Nobody told people they couldn't have steak and chips. The Wizard just created the environment for a new steak, minus the animals, to become the most attractive choice for people. It's classic change theory – build the new, don't fight the old – the Wizard understands that. We still have amazing steak. I'll take you somewhere tonight so you can see for yourself, but if it looks the same, smells the same, tastes the same and is better for you – who cares that it's plant- not animal-based?"

"No one... I guess," says Dorie stuffing the last of her sandwich into her mouth. Her mind is elsewhere now though. Perhaps their dairy farm in Devon really is in trouble this time. She's come all this way to find the Wizard so she can get home to try and save it. She's never questioned if the farm is beyond or, even worth, saving.

"Oh, this came for you this morning," says Glinda, breaking Dorie's thoughts.

Dorie opens a small cardboard box and groans. "Another smartwatch? Really? After what happened yesterday?"

"You'll be fine, you're in the heart of the city now. It's pretty safe here. Just don't stray into any more dark and empty alleys."

"Ah, I was hoping we could spend the day together and you could show me around," says Dorie, a little deflated.

"I'd love to, but I've got to head back out to work. I get off at seven so we can meet then," says Glinda, strapping the watch to Dorie's wrist. She presses something and the screen lights up. "I've programmed it with a route around the city – you might as well see some of it while you wait to see the Wizard. And I've entered the place I'll meet you for dinner tonight – just click on it and it will give you directions to get there from wherever you are – I'll meet you there around 19:15. Any problems, I've put my number in there too."

"Okay," says Dorie, feeling more uplifted again.

"Looks like the Wizard's office has scheduled a call with you at midday so maybe take that here and head out afterwards," suggests Glinda.

"They have?" asks Dorie.

"Yes, but don't get too excited, it's probably just to arrange an appointment for you to meet later in the week. You are welcome to stay here until then."

"Thanks, Glinda," says Dorie. "You go get ready for work; I can clear up here."

***

The watch screen lights up and vibrates against Dorie's arm at 12 noon on the dot. She looks at it and reads 'Great Wizard's Office'. She presses 'accept'.

"Please hold for the Great Wizard," she hears an annoyingly upbeat mechanical sounding voice say. The room gets exceptionally bright as an enormous 3D holographic head is projected from the watch.

"Wow," says Dorie jumping back, the giant head leaping back in tandem with her.

The head smiles. "Surprised by the technology?" it asks, the lips moving in sync with the words.

"No, well yes, but it's just that..." Dorie pauses, her face flushing.

"Go on," says the talking projected head.

"It's just, well, I wasn't expecting the Great Wizard to be a woman." Dorie's cheeks burn more fiercely as she casts her mind back to everyone she's met on her journey and how many times she's referred to the Wizard as a man.

"Haven't you realised that things here are different?" says the Wizard.

"Well yes. On my journey much has seemed familiar, but just as I think I'm experiencing déjà vu, something's different, and it throws me. From the outset, the image in my head for the Great Wizard of Oz was a little old man, with a bald head and a wrinkled face – not a vibrant and stylish younger woman. Sorry."

"There's no need to apologise. But you'd be wise to remember you don't have to change everything in a story to get a different ending. People often think you need a whole new story to bring about change. But you don't. You can create something quite different, by changing and introducing a few key elements."

"I see," says Dorie, although she's not sure she does.

"Great. Well as it happens, I'm in the process of exploring the next of those possible changes for Oz and I was hoping you could help me?" says the Wizard.

"Err, well okay, if you think I can be useful, but I was rather hoping you could help me get home?" says Dorie.

"Maybe we could help each other," responds the Wizard. "I understand you are planning to go sightseeing in the Emerald City this afternoon?" Dorie nods. "Do it, enjoy it," says the Wizard, "but as you explore do so with this question in your mind: 'Should Oz become a cashless society?' If you can come to my office tomorrow afternoon and give me your reflections on that, then I'll help you get home."

"Me? Why would you want my opinion on that? I'm not an economist. I don't know anything about Oz or its monetary system."

"Maybe not," says the Wizard, "but you'll be exploring our city for the first time so will have fresh eyes. You'll have an outside perspective so can be objective. You also don't live here so you can be honest with me and, trust me when I tell you this, honesty is valuable to a leader because it is always difficult to find. And lastly..." The Wizard hesitates, seemingly selecting her next words carefully. "And lastly, I understand your arrival last night to our great city wasn't what we aspire to."

"I got mugged," says Dorie glumly, automatically touching the bruise on the back of her head again.

"Yes, that's very unfortunate but not necessarily unhelpful for the purposes of your task," says the Wizard. "You see we've noticed visitors to the Emerald City are often targeted. We think it's because they arrive with cash and with their smartwatch – which is easily converted into cash. You see cash is becoming much less common in the Emerald City, most people now pay electronically.

Financially it seems to make sense to phase out cash, but these persistent muggings leave an unanswered question in my mind as to whether that's the right thing to do. Then again, maybe if there were no cash, we'd get rid of some of the crime and vice and so improve the reputation of the Emerald City. I'm just not sure, that's why I need your help. If you can help me with this, then I think I can help you get home."

Dorie feels a little overwhelmed by the task but, when the Wizard puts it like that, she can't see that she has much choice.

"Okay," says Dorie reluctantly. "I'll see what I can do but I still think there are others, much better placed than me, to help you with this."

"Great. That's settled then. You come to my office tomorrow lunch time with your thoughts and I'll find a way to get you home. Sorry to be rude but I'm running late for my next meeting, so I need to go. I look forward to meeting you in person tomorrow Dorie." And before Dorie has time to speak, the Wonderful Woman Wizard of Oz has gone, replaced by the symbol:

8 The wonderful Emerald City

"And now if you look to your left, you'll get a great view across the Emerald City," the tour guide tells the bus full of tourists. Dorie isn't sure but she seems to be the only one from completely outside Oz.

"Why's it called the Emerald City?" a young boy asks.

"Because it's like an emerald – both precious and green," the tour guide explains. "This is the greenest city in all of Oz," he says with obvious pride. "We've got the cleanest air, the least waste, it's easy to get around without a car and it's affordable to live here."

"It looks like a maze from here," another visitor comments.

"Actually, it's more like clusters of interconnected mazes. Each is its own community. As more and more come and live here, the city grows organically. It looks a bit messy when you see it from here, but this is the result of millions of decisions by those living, working, and playing here. You'll see when we get down there though, each is a hub of activity – somehow it just works. Before we move on, just look to your right." All heads instinctively turn in unison to look right. "This is how our great city helps feed itself. So much food in Oz is destined for its cities – it just didn't make sense to keep transporting it all from so far away. So, we brought some of the growing closer – you'll find plenty of these types of smaller local farms circling the outskirts of this and increasingly Oz's other cities." No mention of big farms, Dorie can't help but think suspiciously.

As the bus continues onwards, a group of young kids run to the edge of the field waving as they pass. Dorie waves back.

DOI: 10.4324/9781003217657-10

"Ah, our munchkins," says the tour guide noticing Dorie's wave.

"Your what?" asks Dorie.

"Munchkins. It's a term of endearment here in Oz for our youngsters. Schools are now a distributed network of learning hubs, but personal tutors regularly bring their kids out to these nearby farms to help them understand how their food grows. When you see the work involved in growing something, you are much more respectful of it. Together with some helpful tech, this hands-on learning is proving highly effective in reducing how much good food is wasted at home."

As the bus weaves its way into the hubbub of the Emerald City, Dorie is dazzled by its brilliancy. The streets are alive with people walking from place to place, against a backdrop of interwoven apartments, businesses, and green spaces, all powered by a web of renewable energy systems. She listens as the tour guide explains how the entire city is designed and built to cascade energy and materials – to circulate rather than extract value. It certainly seems to be thriving.

"And this," says the tour guide, "is where the wonderful Wizard of Oz works." A towering living wall greets the visitors.

"Wow," says the younger boy from earlier. "It really is green."

"Yes," says the tour guide. "Both inside and out. This living wall is by far the largest in the city holding 1.5 million plants. It looks impressive but it's also cleaning our air. Nature's inspired the building's entire design – we've really been re-thinking how we use and reuse things. Everything is designed to be taken apart when it is no longer needed and reused to create something else – equally as valuable or close to it."

"You're having us on mate, aren't you?" says a burly guy at the back of the bus. "I'm a builder and trust me, if the Wizard decides to relocate this office to where I live in Oz, the far corner of Quadline Country, there's no way it's possible to reuse what goes into this building when it's no longer needed."

"Between imagination, technology and the enabling frameworks – anything is possible in Oz," says the tour guide obviously resorting to his training brief and delivering his spiel without a hint of irony. "Today this is the Wizard's office building. Tomorrow, as you rightly say, it might not be. But if that's understood from the outset, any building, indeed anything, can be designed to be repurposed or taken apart and used again elsewhere."

Dorie can tell from the builder's expression that he's having a hard time believing this, but she can't hang around to see if he leaves the bus convinced. She's exactly where she wants to be now – the place she'll be meeting the Wizard tomorrow. As she stands to leave the bus, the tour guide has started talking about passports, not for people or pets, but for products and materials. This really is a strange land, she thinks, why would anyone go to the trouble of issuing passports for inanimate objects? She doesn't get to hear why, neither does it occupy her thoughts for long because she hops off the bus to suss out what's around the Wizard's office.

***

Having been on the tour bus for what feels like an eternity, Dorie heads around the corner and spots a coffee shop. There's a homeless girl outside, sitting on the pavement. "Spare any change?" the girl asks Dorie as she passes to go inside.

"I haven't got any. I'll break a note inside and get some for you on my way out," she promises the girl.

Dorie orders a tall, extra hot latte and heads to the till to pay. 'We are a cashless café,' states a handwritten note on top of the till.

"Oh," says Dorie as the cashier hands her the latte. "I'm sorry, I didn't realise you were cashless. This is a bit embarrassing, but I'm new to the city and don't have another way to pay – my watch isn't set up to make payments." The cashier snatches the drink back. "You aren't going to let me have it?" asks an astonished Dorie. "I can pay but I only have cash."

"Then you can't pay," says the guy behind the till, "we're a cashless café," he says flatly looking past her at the growing queue. Dorie just stands there looking at him.

The guy behind her has started clicking his tongue impatiently. "I'll pay for her coffee," he says.

"Thanks," says Dorie turning to him with genuine relief and gratitude.

"I just need to get back to work," he says dismissively. "And a double expresso," he says to the cashier.

The guy behind the till passes Dorie her coffee back and waves her away.

"Thanks," she says quietly to no one in particular, as she walks away and towards an empty chair in the corner of the café.

Each time the door swings open and someone new enters, Dorie hears the familiar call of 'spare any change'. Dorie feels for the homeless girl. She has no change to give her and everyone else shakes their head, paying on their smartwatch. It's probably not the best place for the homeless girl to position herself – hoping for change outside a cashless café. But then, where would be good to sit if the entire city went cashless?

As she sips her coffee, Dorie remembers a fly-poster, crookedly slapped to the bus shelter, she'd seen on her bus journey back from work yesterday. It showed a homeless guy sat crossed legged on the floor, just like this girl now. The difference was, poster guy held a sign which read: 'Keep your coins, I want change.' The image was so powerful in its simplicity it had stuck with her. Looking at the scene unfolding here now, Dorie can't help but wonder if either would ever be possible.

***

Dorie is hovering just outside a central bustling square. A sign over the entrance reads: 'Festival of urban food'. She checks her smartwatch. She's in the right place – even if she's having difficulty believing there can be that much to celebrate as far as urban food is concerned. She's also ahead of herself, it's only six o'clock. It will be at least another hour before Glinda gets off work and joins her here.

"You coming in?" says a face Dorie recognises but can't place.

He outstretches his hand. "It's Matt." He waits for a glimmer of recognition. Seeing none, he adds: "The medic from last night."

"Oh yes, of course. This is serendipitous," says Dorie.

"Not really," says medic Matt. "I've been working with Glinda today and we've been keeping an eye on your location. I finished my shift early and when Glinda saw you were already heading this way, she asked me to come and meet you. I was going to join you for dinner tonight anyway and as I only live around the corner..."

"You live right in the heart of the city too?" questions Dorie. "Being a medic must pay a lot more here than it does where I'm from."

"Well, I don't know about that," laughs medic Matt, "but the Wizard has worked her magic on public services and social housing – I've benefited from both."

"You don't own your home then?" Dorie asks.

"No," says medic Matt. "Hardly anyone in the city does. We had to make a choice – it came down to ownership or affordable access. It started with housing, but it goes way beyond that now – this city is built on a service model. Do you own your own home?"

"Yes. No. Well, it's complicated. But your whole city's housing can't be built on rentals?" Dorie says diverting the conversation away from her and back to Oz.

"No not all of it, there are exceptions. Some people still own their own home, but they don't let you borrow too much now and hoarding loads of property or land to rent or sell on for inflated sums, attracts hefty tax penalties."

"Still some hungry land vultures then," says Dorie remembering how the scarecrow had described it.

"Ha! Never heard it put like that before but yes. Still, if I'm being honest, I was pretty against the proposal at the beginning. I'd always wanted to own my home and make a good load of cash for when I retired but that was probably a pipe dream anyway given my career choice. Don't get me wrong, I still think it would be amazing to own my own home, you know, not to have to pay any rent, but now I live in an affordable, comfortable and warm apartment, right in the heart of the best city in Oz, doing a job I love."

"And all it took was a tax change?" says Dorie unconvinced.

"Well, a few actually. It started with land and property but now the Wizard's made it unattractive to make money in Oz from doing nothing – she's all about promoting productivity."

"You sound like you work for the Wizard's marketing team. What does that mean to people like you and me?" asks Dorie.

"Working to make a positive difference is rewarded. Making good money through hard work isn't a problem, but if you go to sleep tonight and wake up much richer in the morning for having done nothing – that is."

"The Wizard's vision is all about giving people access to Oz's communal assets and resources to be productive. They provide the means to secure personal prosperity. Access enables opportunity."

"That's why syphoning off communal assets solely for personal gain or running them out of existence or restricting productivity is heavily disincentivised."

"Well, I'm not likely to do anything like that," says Dorie.

"Exactly," says medic Matt. "That's why the Wizard's been in office for so long. She's popular because people here are mostly like you. She's shifted taxes and fees to make non-renewables and unproductive income unattractive. This is a circular city – it means the focus is on keeping things in circulation. The Wizard taxes things like financial transactions and un-taxes things that are productive and renewable, like green energy or people."

"Hang on a minute. Are you saying you don't pay tax on what you earn as a medic?" Dorie asks incredulously but suddenly extremely interested.

"Not a bean," says Matt smiling. "My work is productive, it adds value to Oz. The Wizard encourages that by taxing those, and those things, that don't do that."

Dorie is thinking about her supermarket payslip and the enormous chunk in the right-hand column that's deducted each month in tax. She'd be rich if she worked here in Oz. The thought of the supermarket leads her mind back to food. She hasn't eaten since Glinda fixed her that sandwich this morning and she's starving. As though reading her mind medic Matt asks: "Shall we?" then, linking arms with Dorie, he leads her into the buzzing festival of urban food.

9 The magical festival of urban food

There is a feast of food stalls, but Matt leads Dorie past them to an enormous open kitchen. It's alive with activity. People are busy sorting, scrubbing, slicing, stirring, simmering, and serving up a wealth of food.

"What is all this? Dorie asks.

"It's community cuisine," says medic Matt. "Oz-style home cooking at its best. You just pitch up and get stuck in. It's a place people come together and connect over food. You eat like a local because it's made by locals. It started out as a project to promote sustainable food and reduce food waste but it's much more than that now. You'll often find great chefs here, working to create recipes with whatever ingredients are available on the day or running cookery workshops. It's social change through gastronomy."

There he goes again, thinks Dorie, sounding like a TV advert but she's genuinely impressed by so many people connecting over food. Maybe Matt the medic missed his vocation, he could have been Matt the marketeer, she thinks. Interrupting her thoughts medic Matt says, "all we have to do is get stuck in."

"You mean, in the kitchen? Oh no I couldn't. I can't cook," says Dorie.

"You can't cook?" says medic Matt disbelievingly. "I thought Glinda said you lived on a farm?"

"I did. I do. It's complicated. It's a dairy farm so that's got nothing to do with cooking, plus we don't do food like this where I'm from. I mean, people connect over cooking *programmes* all

DOI: 10.4324/9781003217657-11

right but most of them are eating their TV dinners as they're watching."

Matt doesn't say anything and throws her an apron. "You've got to be able to peel a carrot," he says.

It turns out to be more than *a* carrot. As they squeeze into the bustling kitchen a guy with a sack truck wheels in five pallets of fresh vegetables. Dorie peers at them.

"They're still dirty," she says.

"Well of course they are," says sack truck guy. "They only got dug out the ground a few hours ago. They've come straight from the farm." Sack truck guy studies her. "You're not from round here are you?"

"You have no idea," laughs Matt the medic as he splinters off from Dorie to take a position further down the kitchen. Ignoring him Dorie asks: "Is all the city's food locally grown then?"

"No not all but a lot."

"How though?" Dorie asks. "Where I'm from, there seems to be this constant battle between global and local. The latter always seems to lose because it's too small, too expensive or both."

The sack truck guy is nodding as she speaks. "The Emerald City and all cities in Oz have been expanding. We had to think about how we were going to feed everyone. And we were wasting so much good food because it was travelling so far. Bringing some growing and processing closer just made sense. The trouble is, us small producers can't supply enough to feed everyone, but when enough of you locally come together to complement rather than compete against a central system, then it works. It's not global versus local, it's both."

Dorie is thinking about her job at the supermarket and life with her Aunt E on their small dairy farm. Could she ever see a future in which the two could work together harmoniously? The sack truck guy must see her contemplation because he continues: "Don't get me wrong, I'm not saying it has been easy. But Oz's big cities have enormous power..."

"...Because they are magical," Dorie says trying to predict the end of his sentence.

"No, because of the volume of food eaten within them. I know it seems obvious, but it took us ages to realise we didn't need to find a way to deal with loads of food waste if we could stop it piling up in the first place. We had to fix our food system – including thinking about food waste in its design. That's taken time, collaboration, investment, smart thinking, tech and a great deal of pressure and patience, but we've got multiple food loops working now, so it's been worth it."

"It certainly seems like it," says Dorie signalling to the buzz of activity all around her. "So, it's less about the Emerald City being a drop off point and more about it being a hub for cultivating, creating and consuming its own food?"

"Exactly," says the sack truck guy clapping his hands together excitedly, clearly happy she's interested and gets it.

"With many local growers and producers, all connected through platform technology, it's just easier now to find local buyers wanting our food or its by-product. We've dramatically reduced wasted food and food waste. All the peelings here tonight, will go back into the food cycle to strengthen the soil. Nothing gets wasted, it just becomes food for something else. And because we're farming this close to the city, people demanded we clean up our practices – so farms and their food are much healthier too."

'Hmm sounds too good to be true. Who pays?' Dorie wonders. She thinks she gets it but now sack truck guy has started talking about by-products and platform technology she thinks it might be time to politely excuse herself and get on with peeling veg, which is exactly what she does.

***

Dorie and medic Matt have already perched themselves at an enormous, communal table with their drinks when Glinda arrives. She's accompanied by a group of friends who all join them.

"Let me get your dinner Dorie," says Glinda: "There's something I really want you to try."

"Thanks," says Dorie. "As long as we can eat soon, I'm starving."

Glinda comes back five minutes later with two plates of food. She puts one in front of Dorie.

"Steak and chips," Dorie laughs.

"Well, FakeSteak but try it," says Glinda.

Dorie is too hungry to even consider protesting. She cuts into it. "Oh, my goodness," gasps Dorie. The table goes quiet and all eyes fix on Dorie. Prodding it with her knife she says: "It's bleeding! I thought you said it wasn't from an animal?"

"It's not," says Glinda. "They create that effect with beetroot juice but it's pretty realistic right?"

"That's incredible and it tastes good," says Dorie through half a mouthful.

The conversation turns from food towards life in the city more generally. Dorie quizzes Glinda's friends about what they do. Some work for private profit companies but others work for themselves, cooperatives, not for profits, charities and, of course, the Wizard's office. They all agree it's much easier to choose where they invest their time since being freed up by the basic dividend.

The broad consensus seems to be that life in the Emerald City is good, but something is nagging away at Dorie. "It can't be all great," she challenges. "I'm here with you tonight because I got mugged and Glinda and Matt helped me. From what I see, for all the good, there's still crime, there's still homelessness on the streets."

"Look, all I can say is this is a big city, it has problems," says the guy sitting opposite her. "The Wizard has made lots of changes, it has made life better but that doesn't, and never will, change human behaviour. Mental health issues don't just disappear; some people reject or simply aren't capable of embracing change; others choose to operate in the shadows. At the end of the day people are still people."

The girl to his right says: "Well maybe if the Wizard upped the basic dividend it would help".

Dorie smiles at that. The guy opposite her isn't wrong. People are still people she thinks. Even when life is good, human nature is to want for more. But more of what and why is it the Wizard who decides how much is enough?

Taking in the wider scene, Dorie spots a group of teenagers huddled around a stall in the far corner. The stall is teetering on the edge of the festival, hidden in the shadows. Dorie is curious, especially since the young crowd are obscuring her view. She watches them. Most are sporting smartwatches but are digging into pockets and rucksacks for cash.

"What's going on over there?" Dorie asks Glinda, who follows her gaze.

"Err cakes," Glinda says, her initial embarrassment falling into a frown.

"They must be good," says Dorie failing to spot Glinda's expression. "Look at that queue. Perhaps I could get us all some for dessert. I've got a little cash left." She pulls the last note from her bra.

There's a nervous laugh from the rest of the table.

"They are magic cakes," says medic Matt.

"Well of course they are," says Dorie flippantly, "everything in Oz is magical right?"

Matt the medic realises Dorie has no idea what he's implying.

"It's the type of magic that messes with your head," Matt adds.

"Oh, you really mean *magic* cakes," says Dorie embarrassed at her naivety. "Is that kind of thing legal here then?"

"It's frowned upon shall we say but not strictly illegal," says Glinda.

"Ah, that's why they are all paying in cash," says Dorie as what she is seeing starts to fall into place.

"Well, who wants that sort of activity on their electronic footprint?" asks medic Matt.

'Who indeed?' Dorie thinks to herself. And it's that question, rather than the festival's food, that fuels Dorie's thoughts as the friends say their goodnights.

10 The nightmare of Oz the Terrible

Safely back in Glinda's apartment, Dorie has fallen into a deep sleep. In her vivid dream, she finds herself in a far-away land, desperately trying to get home but she can't. She is frantically running from place to place trying to get on a bus, a train, a plane – anything that will take her closer to home. But nobody will let her on. She tries to pay for a ticket through her smartwatch, but the ticket machine displays the words 'citizen rating low, travel denied'. She finds a ticket inspector and offers him cash. He simply shakes his head. 'We don't take cash,' he says in the type of slow-motion way that can only happen in a dream. 'Nobody here takes cash.'

Through the crowded train concourse Dorie spots Glinda. She rushes over to her. 'Help me,' she pleads with Glinda, 'I must get home'.

'You did this to yourself. You destroyed your citizen rating through your own actions,' says Glinda harshly. 'Now you are stuck here.'

'But I have to get home. I didn't realise the cakes were magic. Buying them was an innocent mistake. I'm only young, I was naïve. There must be something you can do to help me?'

Glinda looks down at her own smartwatch. 'I have to go,' she says. 'Just being here with you is draining my own citizen rating.' She starts to move away but turns back to call over her shoulder: 'The only thing you can do is go plead your case in front of Oz the Terrible.' And then Glinda is lost to the crowd.

In the next moment, Dorie is in a grand court room. It is dark and oppressive. There is a huge throne like chair on a raised

DOI: 10.4324/9781003217657-12

platform in front of her. The throne is empty but there is a monstrous green head floating above it.

'I am Oz the Terrible,' bellows the disapproving head.

There doesn't seem to be anyone else in the room with them and Dorie is very scared. The Wizard has an ugly distorted face with a single black dead eye.

'I am Dorie' she says meekly 'and I need to get home, but I can't because there has been a mistake'.

'Oz the Terrible does not make mistakes,' booms the enormous green head.

'Of course not,' says Dorie. 'I mean, I made the mistake. I bought something I shouldn't have, by accident. I didn't realise what I was buying. Anyway, now my smartwatch won't work. It won't let me pay for a ticket to get home.'

'Let me check your file,' thunders Oz the Terrible. A mass of data appears from nowhere. It automatically scrolls at an incredibly fast pace, which the head's black dead eye scans through.

'Is that all about me?' Dorie asks surprised by the wealth of information Oz the Terrible has already accumulated about her.

'Quiet!' bellows the green head making Dorie jump. 'I collect this information about everyone because Oz is a special place and I must keep it that way. Your behaviour is not good. So far you have often been a hindrance to our society.'

'I have not,' Dorie protests angrily. 'Who are you to say this?'

'QUIET! No one interrupts Oz the Terrible. You make poor decisions. It's been evident from the moment you got here. You arrived with an alien dog, unaccompanied by the appropriate paperwork, and then illegally sold it on the black market. On reaching the Emerald City, you headed down a dark alley. That led you to needing costly medical assistance. You lost valuable state-owned assets when you had your smartwatch stolen. You've purchased the types of goods that hurt, not help, productive behaviour. It's all here. This is a permanent digital footprint on you. There is nothing to be done, your appeal is denied.'

'But there must be something I can do. I must get home,' says Dorie starting to cry. 'I love Toto, I didn't want to sell him. And those other things, they weren't my fault. Is there someone else I can appeal to?'

'Do you dare to question the decision of the Great Oz the Terrible?'

'No. I mean, yes. I mean, I must get home. I can't stay here stranded.'

'You must redeem yourself and increase your rating. That is the only way. Court adjourned.' The enormous green, monstrous head of Oz the Terrible disappears.

Alone in the throne room, Dorie starts crying uncontrollably. It's hopeless, she thinks. Glinda won't even speak to her, nobody is going to help her, she can't buy anything, she has nowhere to go and no redress. This is a nightmare she thinks. That means it can't be real. Wake up Dorie. WAKE UP.

Dorie opens her eyes to find herself back in Glinda's spare room. Glinda's approaching her bed with a cup of tea.

"I had a dreadful dream," says Dorie.

"I know, I heard," says Glinda. "Meeting the Wizard today is clearly playing on your mind." She pauses, handing Dorie the mug. "Word to the wise though. I wouldn't refer to her as Oz the Terrible. You want her to help you get home remember?"

Glinda smiles and leaves Dorie alone with her mug of tea and her thoughts. It was a terrible dream but now she is awake it seems more like an epiphany. For the first time, Dorie is confident about what she will say to the Wizard in response to her cashless country challenge.

11 Meeting the wonderful Wizard of Oz

Dorie steps across the threshold into the Wizard's towering office block. It's much brighter and airier inside than she imagined it would be, given the enormity of the exterior green wall. The building has a glass atrium flooding the grand entrance with natural light, which also reflects off an indoor stream, complete with fish.

Dorie is nervous and excited as she approaches the visitor's area but not so much so that she fails to notice the magnificent mosaic floor. It depicts the Emerald City and prominently features the numbers:

DOI: 10.4324/9781003217657-13

These numbers spark a glimmer of recognition within Dorie. She knows they are familiar but why? It stays just out of her reach. By the time she's ushered through the hubbub of people milling around and into a lift, up to the Wizard's office, the mosaic floor and its numerical symbol are all but forgotten to her.

"Dorie," says a welcoming, slender, woman with auburn bobbed hair in a sharp trouser suit walking towards her with the support of a cane, "welcome to Oz."

"Thanks," says Dorie her voice wavering as her nerves get the better of her. If the Wizard notices the quiver in her voice, she doesn't say anything.

"So how are you enjoying our beautiful land?" the Wizard asks as the pair wander over to the window to survey the Emerald City sprawling below.

"Compared to where I'm from, I'd have to say Oz is amazing," Dorie responds.

"And yet you are here to see me because you are keen to get home?" the Wizard quizzes her.

"I must. For my Aunt E. You see she has a small dairy farm and it's the only life she knows. But things haven't been going so well for us lately and I think the bank is foreclosing on the mortgage and she's going to lose it. She's always done so much for me, I really need to get back there. She needs me now."

"Perfectly understandable and very commendable," says the Wizard. "I think I can help you, but I believe we had an agreement – that you would also help me. So first tell me Dorie, what are your thoughts about our precious circular city going cashless?"

"Don't do it," Dorie blurts out. "What I mean is the evidence I have is that it would be a profound mistake."

"You sound pretty sure for someone who this time yesterday thought they weren't the best person to help me with my dilemma," says the Wizard, somewhat surprised by the strength of Dorie's conviction.

"I know," says Dorie, "but you have created something special in Oz and I think if you take cash away it will work against the strong element of freedom you seem to be creating for your people. You've created this amazing basic dividend which gives people autonomy but so does cash – you don't want to give with one hand and take away with the other."

"But what has cash to do with freedom?" the Wizard questions.

"Cash is a right to citizenship, it's foundational to democracy and it's the economy's safety net that lets everyone participate. Without it you force everything to become digital, every transaction trackable. That will exclude too many. Even if you could find a way to include everyone, they will all have a permanent, financial-digital footprint. People aren't perfect, but cash represents their right to be forgotten. Freedom is being able to spend your money on what you want, when you want, without worrying that something you buy today will be held against you tomorrow."

"But I don't intend to hold people's purchases against them Dorie," the Wizard says.

"I believe you. Those I've spoken to tell me you are a good Wizard, that's why you've been in office so long. But you will not hold this role forever and what if your successor is less scrupulous? What if some future Wizard ties together a person's location from their smartwatch, with what they see, search for, and say through their other digital devices, then link this to their financial transactions and bank account information? Together, that information creates a comprehensive profile. Let's say your less scrupulous successor scores every citizen's profile. With only a digital way to pay for anything, what would stop them, on a whim, deciding a person's score is too poor to access their only digital method of payment – then what?"

"Hmm," says the Wizard, "your concerns are valid but fewer and fewer use cash here, so clearly they aren't too worried about that."

"Maybe they don't yet understand the potential threat. And right now, we're discussing a theoretical future with a less scrupulous Wizard. But what if the joining of those digital dots weren't conducted by a Wizard in Oz, holding public office at all, but by a wicked witch working only for excessive private profit? Say this witch is already a genius in a land far outside Oz with a global digital empire. What or who could stop her shutting down a person's digital presence here and disrupting their entire life? She might use all that digital information to manipulate people without them ever knowing – not only to influence what they buy, but what they believe. She could even introduce her own rival private digital currency – a global one – not that difficult once yours has gone digital. You'll have lost control. And, when things go wrong and your people seek you out for help, all your polite pleas and political potions won't be powerful enough to conjure her to fly into Oz to sort them out with you."

The Wizard's forehead has developed a deep crease in it from her worried frown. Dorie can see she thinks her arguments have merit, so she keeps going, finishing what she wants her to take away. "Anyway, a downward trend in cash transactions doesn't mean everyone has stopped using it," Dorie thinks about the technophobic older gatekeeper, the homeless girl, and the scene at last night's food festival. "Where I'm from most people have a car and drive, but I don't. Hardly anyone uses the bus but if it weren't there I couldn't get to work. A drop in demand doesn't make something any less vital to those who still depend on it. Removing cash is like cutting a public service. Plus, you are the Great Wizard of *Oz* – of all its lands and people. I walked through your countryside to get here and the dwindling amount of cash was already problematic for one rural community – so much so they'd introduced their own complementary community coinage. It seemed to be working pretty well too, solving the local cash and credit problem, and increasing local spending."

"That's very interesting and news to me," says the Wizard, "but it doesn't change the fact that less demand means cash is becoming more costly to keep in circulation."

"I get it, cash costs," says Dorie. "You already know it cost me personally when I got mugged for it when first arriving in the Emerald City. I suspect the only reason they didn't get away with any is because I had it hidden in my bra. What you don't know, and I'm not particularly proud of, is that a lack of cash also cost me my little dog, Toto. I had to sell him to get some to enable my journey to the Emerald City. That's kept me going since my arrival but here in the city simply buying a coffee with cash proved difficult."

The Wizard looks surprised by these revelations but says nothing.

"Look, my point is," continues Dorie, "what starts as an idea about something purely financial, even if it's philanthropic, could be manipulated at a later point in time to restrict wider freedoms. If the price of democracy, autonomy and freedom in Oz is a little inefficiency and cost - surely it has to be worth it?"

Dorie surprises herself with her words and the passion with which she says them. Perhaps she's been in Oz for too long – she's seen this advocacy in others she has met here, but this isn't something she's seen in herself until now. The Wizard, however, seems extremely pleased with her response.

"What I don't understand though," Dorie continues, "cash or cashless, how can you pay for everything you are doing in Oz? The basic dividend, renewable energy, untaxing human labour, social housing, affordable rents, investment in the city's public services and infrastructure – how is it possible to have such an amazing country without going bankrupt?"

"Come with me," smiles the Wizard.

The pair walk to the far end of the Wizard's office. She pulls back a panel built into the wall. Hidden behind is a heavy sealed door. The Wizard looks at a security screen, which scans her face. The door makes a buzzing sound and the Wizard pushes it open. Dorie feels the chill from the air conditioning in the room beyond and hears a low hum. At the flick of a switch, bright light floods the room and Dorie follows the Wizard inside.

"What's all this?" Dorie asks.

"It's a data storage centre," replies the Wizard. "These servers store and process all the digital information circling through Oz."

"And what's so special about that then?" Dorie asks.

"This is where our artificial intelligence is analysing what's happening in Oz in real time and creating the money we need to encourage production. It's circular; the more productive capacity we have the more credit we can extend to encourage more production."

"You are creating money from here?" Dorie questions. "But how is that possible? You are a politician, not a bank."

"I'm the highest elected representative responsible for this land. That means it's within my gift to determine who creates the money," says the Wizard. She carries on, "And money, Dorie, is a public utility. Managing it is like operating any other public service. In Oz, for a long time, that money management was outsourced to private banks. But that model simply stopped working. Money was lent for the wrong things and stopped circulating – it was being unproductively stockpiled by fewer and fewer people. That wasn't good for Oz or its people, it's not what money is designed to do. Money must flow. To create prosperity, everything within our economy must be productive – people, products, property, and pounds. Money especially, must be used and exchanged to circulate and build prosperity. That stopped happening under the management of the private banks and, as Oz has its own currency, there was nothing to stop me taking back its control and creating whatever money the country needed."

"You just took control and started printing your own money? But what about inflation and price rises?" Dorie says in astonishment. "No disrespect but where I'm from governments aren't good at that."

"Well, it may be their thinking is still back to front. When I took charge of this beautiful land, I was told I couldn't spend more than I raised from taxes or borrowed, which added a burden of interest to the future and wasn't true. If I manage all the money, I can produce whatever Oz needs. I know I'm a Wizard, and call me a humbug if you like, but this isn't magic, I simply spend into existence the money that's needed first and tax it back afterwards. When prices start to rise, I adjust taxes."

"Look, I'm just an ordinary girl so the workings of money, even my own, are confusing to me but I think I kind of get it. What I still don't understand though is how you can be so generous? Paying a basic dividend, a welfare safety net, investment in public services – those must cost a lot and yet those I've spoken to here don't even pay tax on their wages. Regardless of whether you raise it before or after spending, where on earth do you get the money to pay for everything?"

"That's like asking where you get inches. You are forgetting Oz creates and controls its own money. We create whatever we need and then heavily tax anything undesirable. That's anything that prevents productivity or the circulation of wealth, harms our land, or we need to keep prices steady. But it isn't just about what I raise in taxes, it's also about what I no longer must pay out," says the Wizard. She can see Dorie's attention waning, so she tries a different tack.

"Let me give you an example," the Wizard continues. "You spoke about our basic dividend. These servers hold a central bank account for everyone in Oz – their basic dividend gets paid into it. As you rightly say that costs, but it also saves money on administering many welfare and pension payments. Do you have any idea how much it costs to means test things? The basic dividend replaces some of those payments and reduces means testing – lessening bureaucracy and cost. The dividend also ensures people have money to spend. Businesses need customers Dorie. The dividend helps keep the economy thriving by generating spending power."

The Wizard turns to glance at Dorie and seeing she still has her interest continues: "But it isn't any one thing that helps, it's the combination of a few – all positively reinforcing each other. When you start combining those, you get a benefit because you've got more people spending on things that help, not harm, Oz and its economy."

"Well, when you put it like that, it sounds pretty straightforward, but I don't think any of this would ever be possible in my land," says Dorie as the pair walk back into the Wizard's main office and the heavy door slams behind them. The Wizard indicates for Dorie to sit in a chair opposite her. "Everything is so mucked up, it's like we're operating in permanent crisis. I can't see how we could ever pull it back to recreate something like you've created here."

"Hmm," ponders the Wizard. "Your land looks democratic... is it not?"

Dorie hesitates but nods as she offers, "once in a while".

The Wizard smiles and continues, "your land has its own, stable, currency does it not?" Dorie nods again. "Then your land has everything it needs to recreate what we have here in Oz."

Dorie doesn't look convinced.

"Look," continues the Wizard, "your input into my cash dilemma has really helped me. I'm grateful for your passion and honesty about it. You've helped me see an invisible yet intrinsic link between democracy and money – both physical and digital. On reflection, I don't think helping you get home is enough in return, especially if things are as bad as you say they are back there. What kind of Wizard would I be if I let you return empty handed, without the ability to better your lot? So, I'm going to sweeten the deal."

Dorie is suddenly very interested, giving the Wizard her full attention. Nobody ever sweetens a deal once made where she is from, but she's not about to tell the Wizard that.

"Go on," says Dorie, trying hard not to give away her surprise and excitement.

"Oz's success is built on a secret works called *The Wonderful Circles of Oz*," says the Wizard. "You've probably seen this symbol displayed around the city." The Wizard indicates towards a photo on the wall that shows:

"That underpins *The Wonderful Circles of Oz*. I'm afraid I'm not going to have the time to go into it in detail now, I've got a meeting with the Council of the Elders, but conceptually it's straight forward."

Checking her smartwatch the Wizard rushes through a statement she's so familiar with, it's clear to Dorie she must have said it a thousand times: "The zero's circular shape signifies our living planet. The one represents the economic process that's forever entwined with our planet's circular, living systems. The two stands for a pair of interconnected cycles that are set in motion during the economic process – the first being materials and the second asset-based. And the fourth, well that's the minimum number of rules each of those cycles need to start working well for society."

"So, sorry, what is it you are giving me?" Dorie asks, completely baffled.

"I'm giving you a choice Dorie," says the Wizard, getting up and walking to her desk to pull two rucksacks from underneath it. One is red, the other blue. "You can leave with one of these two rucksacks. The blue one contains £350,000 in cash – it should be enough to pay the outstanding mortgage on your Aunt E's dairy farm."

"Wow." Dorie can't help herself. The word falls out of her mouth and her jaw drops open in complete surprise. She's never seen that kind of money in her life and the Wizard is offering it to her for a little advice? "What's in the red rucksack?" she asks.

"All the detail behind *The Wonderful Circles of Oz* – everything you need to recreate a version of what you have seen here in Oz once you get back home," says the Wizard.

"That's not a choice," says Dorie. "There's no way anyone from my land could recreate Oz based on a simple formula. I choose the blue rucksack containing all the cash please," Dorie says confidently.

"Let me just show you something before you rush your decision," says the Wizard. She heads over to a cabinet and brings back a board with four metronomes on it. "Do you know what these are?"

"Sure," says Dorie. "They set a beat to help your timing when playing music."

"Exactly right. Now set them going one at a time," says the Wizard. Dorie does as the Wizard instructs, and each metronome begins ticking out its own beat.

"You see how these are all beating out of sync and competing for your attention?" says the Wizard. "This is what Oz used to be like. Lots of good things happening individually but working against each other. The overall effect – messy. Now look what happens when I do this."

The Wizard produces two empty drinks cans, laying them down on their sides, parallel to each other, a hand's width apart. Then, she carefully picks up the board of four metronomes and balances it on the two cans. Both cans begin to gently rock from side to side, just a tiny fraction and then, as if by magic, the metronomes begin to sync, until all four are tapping out a strong harmonious beat and all within about 30 seconds.

"Ha," says Dorie. "That's brilliant. I've never seen that done before. But what does it mean?"

"It means that in discovering and using the right enabling conditions, it can be quick and easy to effect change. It means it's possible to work with what you've got, even if it is a bit of a mess right now, that you don't need to start over to resynchronise. It means you don't necessarily need to change too much to harmonise a system and secure a different result. And it means it's the feedback that's important when you change a few of the right interconnecting things. My point, Dorie, is what underpins *The Wonderful Circles of Oz* is simple but, as you've seen for yourself while you've been here, it works. The formula isn't perfect, Oz isn't perfect, there's always more that can be done but what's in the red bag would go a long way towards helping your entire land."

Dorie suddenly feels a huge burden of responsibility. £350,000 will change hers and Aunt E's life forever. *The Wonderful Circles of Oz,* on the other hand, might better the lives of so many. She knows it would be selfish to take the cash and adopt an 'I'm all right Jack' attitude but, come on, it's £350,000 in cash with no strings attached. And anyway, who else is ever going to know that she took the cash? What they don't know won't hurt them. Dorie takes a deep breath trying to clear her head.

"I'd know," she says aloud talking to her thoughts.

"You'd know what? asks the Wizard.

"I'd know that by taking the rucksack full of cash I'll be letting everyone down, even though they'd never be any the wiser. I met a lion on my way into the Emerald City. He'd done some good things in his community, but he could have done much more. I was quick to judge him for not having the courage to push himself out of his comfort zone. He was good but he might have been great. As it turns out, he didn't have the courage to try, so he stayed put. And yet, now I'm here, faced with that dilemma myself – to be courageous or stick with the safety of what I know I find myself drawn to taking the bag full of cash."

"So, you still want the blue bag full of cash?" the Wizard asks, lifting it up.

Dorie pauses and scrunches up her face. "No," she says tensely. "I'll take the red one containing your *Wonderful Circles of Oz* work," she finishes, albeit somewhat reluctantly.

If the Wizard is pleased with her choice, she doesn't show it. She simply drops the blue rucksack to the floor, which thuds upon impact. She picks up the red one and throws it over to Dorie who, upon catching it, can't help but notice it's incredibly light. 'Oh, I really hope I've done the right thing,' she thinks.

"Well, I'm sorry to break this up, I've really enjoyed meeting you Dorie," says the Wizard, "but I've got to get to my next meeting, and you need to get home."

"You can get me home right now?" Dorie beams.

"It will take some time for you to reach your destination but, yes, I can get you on your way right now," the Wizards says. "Speak to my assistant on the way out. I've arranged for the self-driving Tesla I lease to take you home."

"You mean I could have driven home at any time?" Dorie asks incredulously.

"Well theoretically yes. Obviously, you'd have needed the right car to get you across the desert between Oz and where you call home, but don't you worry, the car has successfully crossed the toughest desert."

"But if it was that simple, why didn't you just arrange for your car to collect me when we spoke yesterday? Or why didn't anyone on my journey tell me it was possible to cross the desert and get home that way?" Dorie says, more than a little miffed.

"But had that happened," says the Wizard, "you wouldn't have been able to help me with my cashless dilemma and neither would you be returning home with *The Wonderful Circles of Oz*. You are leaving with everything you need, Dorie, not to save your aunt's farm but to save your country."

Dorie laughs out loud. "I can't go home and save my country. I'm just an ordinary girl. I work in a supermarket and help on a farm filled with cows."

"But you've chosen the red rucksack," says the Wizard somewhat confused. "What are you planning to do with *The Wonderful Circles of Oz* then?"

"Honestly? I was going to send it to Downing Street – that's where all the big decisions are made about our country."

"Dorie, you can't just post it on and hope someone picks it up and runs with it. You've seen what this looks like in practice. You've got to go home and paint a vivid picture of what's possible. You've got to get people rallied around *The Wonderful Circles of Oz* as a starting point for a way to get there."

"But I can't do that. I don't know the first thing about our country's politics or its economy and I'm not a Wizard. There are people better placed than me to do this type of thing."

"Like there were people better placed than you to advise me on whether or not Oz should become cashless?" The Wizard lets the statement hang for a moment. "Don't you get it yet Dorie? You don't need to be a politician, an economist, or a Wizard – you just need to be involved. Democracy is a participatory sport. Go home Dorie. Tell your story of Oz. Help your people see that creating something better is neither impossible nor fictional."

***

And that is all the Wizard has to say because someone interrupts her and whisks her off to her next meeting.

The Wizard's assistant escorts Dorie back to the lift, which this time descends to a basement level car park. Dorie's then bundled into the Tesla, together with her red rucksack. Nobody lines the streets to wave her off and, with her destination pre-programmed, she doesn't even get the chance to say goodbye to her host, Glinda.

Without needing to drive herself, Dorie thinks about everything she's seen in Oz. She watches the scenery roll by until her eyes grow heavy and she nods off. She has no idea how long she's been asleep, but she's woken by an automated voice telling her she has 'reached her destination'. With that, her door pops up and opens like that of a spaceship. Dorie sleepily grabs her red rucksack and stumbles out towards Aunt E's farmhouse.

12 Back home

Aunt E hadn't noticed Dorie's extended absence. Dorie couldn't help herself though, she was excited to be home, and rushed in to greet her aunt with an enormous bear hug.

"I've missed you," Dorie said, "and I've got so much to tell you."

"Get off me, silly girl," Aunt E said in a kindly way. She was clearly quietly pleased by Dorie's spontaneous show of affection. "You can tell me everything over dinner."

"Great, I'm starving," replied Dorie. "How long?"

Aunt E headed over to the fridge and yanked out two ready-meals. She speared the top of each with a fork and put them in the microwave, setting the timer to six minutes. While waiting for it to ting off, she headed back to the fridge and pulled out a half-empty bottle of Chardonnay and poured two generous glasses. She placed them on the table and then emptied the contents of both microwave meals onto plates, plonking one down in front of Dorie. Sitting directly opposite her, Aunt E asked: "So, what's all this you've got to tell me?"

Dorie was suddenly nervous. Where should she start? She decided it was probably best just to start at the beginning and tell her Aunt E everything.

Dorie cut into her chicken, but it was like rubber. She cut a lump off and when Aunt E headed over to the fridge to retrieve the rest of the wine, Dorie dropped the chicken on the floor. Then she remembered she no longer had Toto to rely on to eat it. She decided it might be an idea to skip the part of the story where she sold Toto.

DOI: 10.4324/9781003217657-14

Aunt E was much enjoying her tale, at least right up until the point where she found out Dorie didn't take the blue rucksack stuffed with cash.

"You did what?" Aunt E said, her eyes open wider than Dorie had ever seen them. "Someone offered you enough cash to save the farm and you turned it down?"

"I know it sounds a bit crazy, but *The Wonderful Circles of Oz* is special," flushed Dorie. "I saw it working in practice so I know it can work. It can help a lot of people, not just us. I thought you'd be proud of me, that you'd think I made the right choice."

"Some stupid formula, over our farm, our home, our livelihood?" screamed Aunt E, jumping from her chair, which screeched loudly against the dull, flagstone floor. It was a long time since Dorie had seen her aunt this angry. "What an earth is wrong with you girl? Philanthropy is for the rich, not people like us."

Dorie pushed her plate aside. She knew there was only one way to calm her aunt who was glaring down at her accusingly with her hands firmly welded to her hips, and that was to show her why taking *The Wonderful Circles of Oz* was overwhelmingly the right decision. But Dorie hadn't even looked at what the Wizard had given her yet. Her choice had seemed so logical when she was in Oz but right here and now, confronted with her aunt's wrath, she was beginning to doubt herself.

Reluctantly Dorie pulled the rucksack onto the table and, with shaking hands, opened it. Inside she found an A4 envelope with an Emerald Green wax seal over the opening. Dorie ripped it open pulling out a dog-eared, roughly bound document. The words '*The Wonderful Circles of Oz*' printed in large bold font across the cover. The cover also hosted, somewhat ironically Dorie thought, a perfectly circular coffee stain. It was not, however, the professionally presented book she'd hoped to impress her aunt with.

"That's it?" said Aunt E, grabbing it from her and flicking through it. "You've got to be kidding me? This is a joke, it's a complete mess. Look at all this," Aunt E pointed to a section that had been scribbled out, then turning a page she said "and this,"

indicating to some handwritten notes in the margin. "Clearly, your Wizard hasn't even finished it."

"It's not set-in stone," Dorie said jumping to the Wizard's defence. "This is real life, things evolve, progress is ongoing. It makes sense that the Wizard would be constantly updating it and Oz is a democracy, she's not pulling it together single-handedly. There's probably been loads of people working on this document."

"Dorie, even if that were true, how are you ever going to make head or tail of this lot? This isn't Jack and the bloody beanstalk, as you just said yourself, this is real life, with real-world consequences," Aunt E was shouting again. "Get your butt outside, get back in that fancy car you said brought you here, go back to the Wizard and say you're sorry, you made a mistake, you've changed your mind and get the bag containing the cash."

"I don't think it works like that Aunt E," said Dorie glumly. Still, she got up from the table and followed her aunt outside. But, as Dorie knew it would be, the Tesla was long gone.

13 Chasing rainbows

Everything was stormy. The weather, the financial markets, and Dorie's relationship with her Aunt E. Dorie had been continually feeling bad for what her aunt had, on more than one occasion, referred to as 'the stupidity of her decision'. Neither her aunt's reprimands nor Dorie's reaction of frequent self-loathing, stopped the removals van arriving to take their furniture away and Aunt E with it.

Before leaving, Aunt E told Dorie: "I love you, but I'm so upset at losing the farm. I know it's not your fault but, for now, I just need some space."

"I understand," said Dorie and, not wanting to strain their relationship further, she told her aunt, "don't worry about me, I'm going to stay with some friends for a while." That was a small white lie to protect her aunt's feelings though. The thought of sofa surfing was simply too much for Dorie to bear right then and she was really going to stay with her Uncle Hen, who had a tiny apartment in Exeter City. Dorie adored her Uncle Hen but sadly her aunt didn't anymore, which was why the pair were no longer together.

The landlord didn't allow substantial changes to be made to the apartment, but Uncle Hen had devised an ingenious temporary partition dividing the living space in two, so she had her own bedroom. It was just big enough for Dorie to squeeze a single bed and a chest of drawers into. The walls were flimsy but it was private and Dorie much appreciated the gesture.

She had been there a few months when Uncle Hen arrived home one afternoon to find Dorie still in her PJs watching Judge

DOI: 10.4324/9781003217657-15

Judy. “Dorie, that’s it, I’ve been patient but you can’t just lounge about on my sofa all day, every day.”

“But Uncle Hen, I’ve tried,” Dorie protested.

“Then try harder or try something, anything, else,” said Uncle Hen. “I can’t stand to see you lolling around, it’s such a waste, you are capable of so much more.”

Dorie wasn’t sure exactly what it was that Uncle Hen had said but she realised he was right. She couldn’t sit unproductively on her butt for the rest of her life. What was it she was so scared of anyway? She had already lost so much – what else did she have left to lose? For the first time since her bust up with Aunt E, she was drawn to *The Wonderful Circles of Oz*. Dorie didn’t say anything, because she realised, she hadn’t even read it yet – it was buried at the bottom of her underwear drawer. But she was suddenly, if not somewhat inexplicably, secretly excited by the hope it might offer.

“You’re right Uncle Hen,” she responded as she jumped from the sofa. “I think there’s something better I could be doing.” Without elaborating any further, Dorie disappeared into her room to dig out *The Wonderful Circles of Oz* and started reading...

14 Official correspondence of The Wizard's Office, Oz

Dear Dorie,

If you are expecting a recipe book, I'm afraid I'm going to disappoint. What you get is this Imaginary. It's my guide detailing the past, present, and future of all our thoughts for building something better or, if we dare to dream, something great.

As we discussed, the core framework is:

It works like the rules of football – the parameters that guide the game. A framework is never the thing itself, just as a map isn't a territory. To know a territory, you must be there. You need the map to avoid getting lost and wasting time. Perhaps some aimless wandering upon arrival is pleasant but it quickly gets

DOI: 10.4324/9781003217657-16

frustrating – particularly if conditions take a turn for the worse. You know all this of course but it's easy to forget how much it matters deep down. You reminded me that the human spirit and variability is itself important. So much is important in itself and yet we forget there is a value in existence and diversity – not just in exchange and efficiency.

This Imaginary has been written many times and one day will be gone. 'This too will pass,' as the ancients said. Change is the only constant. An Imaginary is never complete. It's like Wikipedia in that respect, constantly evolving and totally dependent on many to update it – to be useful and remain relevant.

Within Oz, this is a living document but, when you are back home Dorie, you'll need to make it relevant for your land, your people, your context. Working through it to do so will feel a challenge but that is good. For what is worth anything without part of ourselves invested?

But once you have done it Dorie, you'll find a way to tell your story of Oz. It might help your people not only reimagine but rebuild towards a better future. There always needs be such a story. Without it, civilisation will degrade and destroy itself once more. And every generation must renew it afresh for if there is destiny it is simply this.

It is unlikely we'll meet again, but I hope you'll remember me, as I will you, and that you'll allow Oz to inspire you. Oh, and Dorie, do remember to enjoy this journey you are on from time to time.

Yours, Oz

Part two

A real-world framework. An imaginary for the 21st century.

Updated version based on the Wizard's working guide. Drafted back in Exeter by (Dorie), Ken, & Alex

15 An introduction to this 'Imaginary for today's real world' from Ken & Alex

Author and philosopher Yuval Noah Harari in his book *Sapiens: A Brief History of Humankind* (Harari, 2015) insists that change in society comes through the emergence of narratives that become acceptable rather than strictly testable. Change, firstly, requires these narratives to be better than those we have now.

In similar vein *Narrative Economics*, Robert Shiller (2019) shows how stories with recurring themes have impacted markets. He urges economists to 'pay attention to stories to predict, prepare for, and lessen the damage of financial crises, recessions, depressions and other economic events.'

Stories then, can change our perspectives on life and change our economic behaviour. But what happens when all those stories collectively suggest that our overarching narrative, societal contract, and economic system, no longer hold true? What if our umbrella economy no longer connects to the overarching story it promised?

'To a worm in horseradish, the world is horseradish,' says journalist and author, Malcolm Gladwell (2004). Right now, we know there is a world beyond the horseradish jar constraining us, but imagining it feels impossible.

Storytelling legend, Jonah Sachs, believes stories hold so much societal sway there is currently a hidden war going on to control them. 'We live in a world that's lost its connection to its traditional myths, now we're grasping for new ones. These myths will shape our future, for through story we can help people connect with solutions to complex economic, social and environmental challenges.' Those who can imagine and spread these solutions

DOI: 10.4324/9781003217657-18

by telling the best stories, stories that inspire people to think differently, will win, what Sachs terms, 'the story wars' (Sachs, 2012, pp. 6–7). His book '*Winning the Story Wars*' (Sachs, 2012) is an easy read and excellent resource for telling stickier stories.

Many great stories stem from 'what if'. Our story is no different. We began by asking: What if we could imagine a society beyond the constraints of our current system. What if, just like we discovered with *The Wonderful Wizard of Oz*, we could reflect on ideas long forgotten that might help an alternative narrative emerge? What if that narrative resonates more closely with people and their reality today? Surely, it could create not episodic economic events but wide-scale, systemic change to society and the economy that supports it?

What follows in the remainder of this book is the reimagining of a real-world society worth fighting for – beyond the constraints of our current system, together with a contemporary pathway for how to help move us towards it.

Before diving into the full detail of how we got there though, we first offer an overview of a framework, its system assumptions, and how to approach resetting the rules of the game.

References

Gladwell, M. (2004). *Choice, Happiness and Spaghetti Sauce*. Talk given at TED2004. February 2004 [online]. Available at https://www.ted.com/talks/malcolm_gladwell_choice_happiness_and_spaghetti_sauce?language=en [Last accessed 09 May 2021].

Harari, Y. N. (2015). *Sapiens: A Brief History of Humankind*. London: Vintage.

Sachs, J. (2012). *Winning the Story Wars: Why Those Who Tell – And Live – The Best Stories Will Rule the Future*. Boston, MA: Harvard Business Review Press.

Shiller, R. (2019). *Narrative Economics: How Stories Go Viral and Drive Major Economic Events*. Princeton, NJ: Princeton University Press.

16 An overview

The Wonderful Circles of Oz framework and sigil for resetting the rules of the game

Within our living planet, powered by the abundant flow of energy from the sun, sits our economy. We signify the planet with a **Zero** – reflecting its circular shape. We symbolise the zero with the ancient circular Ouroboros (dragon/snake) endlessly eating its tail to illustrate the planet's ongoing change and renewal.

Our economy is **ONE** dynamic process that's forever entwined with and impacts all the planet's cyclical, living systems.

Our economy sets in motion **TWO** interconnected cycles:

A **productive cycle** endlessly transforms useable energy and materials into useful goods and services before becoming waste. That waste then either flows through (energy) or becomes food (materials) for the system. Wedded to knowledge, technology and powered by an adequate flow of energy, drawn

DOI: 10.4324/9781003217657-19

principally from the sun, this cycle builds capitals and maintains them. In this cycle, money is a medium of exchange and, via savings, a source of productive investment with prices acting as messages. Just as materials need to cleanly flow and remain uncontaminated to become food for the next cycle, so too must prices. Prices need to reflect 'true costs' to do their job.

Many mistakenly believe this productive cycle is the totality of our economy because it is what we hear most about. But our economy also involves a second cycle. We're calling it the **gatekept cycle**, but you may also hear it referred to by others as the 'tollbooth economy' or 'FIRE sector' (Finance Insurance and Real Estate). This is an asset-based cycle that revolves around the ownership and control of commonwealth resources (minerals, land, fossil fuels, and other of the Earth's endowments) and the supply of money as credit. These are two of the critical means of enabling production, exchange, and deciding who benefits. By means of example, when commonwealth assets become privately controlled, access to them and wealth generated from them aren't available to (or managed by) a community of users or Commoners – hence the idea of there being a gate keeper or 'tollbooth' denying or charging for access. In return for that, enclosure is supposed to be a social contract with its roots in mutuality.

We call it the Gatekept cycle

The 'Guardian of the Gates' is a character in Baum's original story. It is this Gate Guardian that grants Dorothy and her companions' passage into the Emerald City and determines whether they will be granted access to see the Great Oz.

Gatekeeping is now also a well-established communications theory about how we access information (Wikipedia, 2021). It was coined in relation to the mass media and how the decisions of one reporter, one news outlet, would determine (through intentional and/or unintentional filtering) the flow of information to the many.

Given the critical role knowledge plays in today's economy and the link to the original story, gatekeeping felt an important theme and so 'Gatekept' seemed an apt descriptor for this cycle. It is easy to visualize a gatekeeper regardless of whether we are talking about:

- A person physically guarding a gate in the real world to charge for or deny access to something, or
- An avatar, protecting what lays beyond a digital paywall in our virtual world.

And, as we see in Dorie's encounter with the gate "greeter" at the gates to Oz, the charge for access no longer necessarily requires us handing over money but frequently something far more valuable – our personal data.

Together the productive and gatekept cycles comprise our economy. It's that economy, that's embedded in our environment and society. Like all the planet's living systems our economy does not exist in isolation, it is nested and as a condition of its enduring character it must be circulatory in nature.

A circular economy is dynamic but adaptive. When enduring, it is effective. It neither courts disaster by over-extending efficiency (brittleness), nor is it too resistant to change (stagnation). That is determined by the system conditions or the rules of the game and to reset those, we suggest four change principles to each of the economy's interconnected cycles as a minimum number required to start the deeper processes of change, to get them working well for society.

FOUR change principles for the productive cycle:

First: Regenerate and restore capitals including natural and social capital. The aim is always wealth creation by building and maintaining stocks. A stock of accessible solutions as entrepreneur and venture capitalist, Nick Hanauer might describe wealth (Hanauer and Beinhocker, 2014).

Second: Be biomimetic. This is the notion that by seeing everything as food for the next cycle, we design out waste (waste = food). This is how all living systems deal with change. It is imagining a 'nutrient economy' (Webster, 2016).

Third: Shift from selling goods to selling services or performance. That vastly extends value because we can access the benefit goods provide, time after time.

Fourth: Celebrate diversity and optimise the whole system. That means diversity of scale, culture, place, connection, and time. A dynamic system is full of change and to thrive it requires diversity. Diversity is strength. It is a fount of creative adaption and a means of resilience. The entire system must have diversity in abundance to be *effective* and optimised rather than *efficient* and brittle.

Energy flows through everything described in these four change principles. This energy use must be renewable in source and optimised.

FOUR change principles to the Gatekept cycle:

First: Create an adequate basic dividend, together with greater access to more historical and newly created commons – a fair share of the surplus coming from enclosed commonwealth resources that exist to benefit everyone. These might include shares/stock for employees, payments for the use of an individual's data, a carbon allowance to add equity to dealing with climate challenges. This helps rebalance the lack of mutuality to the social contract for common inheritance and its private exploitation. This dividend becomes a reality through, among other things, a shift in taxes or fees payable from a myriad of sources. A basic dividend is not dependent though on any one fee, tax, or measure in isolation.

Second: Shift taxes or fees towards non-renewables and away from people and the profits from the productive economy. It's rebalancing the financial and productive economies to:

- Promote and enable equity
- Disincentivise some activities – including waste
- Promote other activities – such as local production.

Third: Relieve people of much of their debt burden with a debt jubilee. In his book *Between Debt and the Devil* (Turner, 2017), the former Chairman of Britain's Financial Services Authority, Adair Turner, describes debt as a kind of financial pollution. Ignoring it is like ignoring carbon already released into the atmosphere – you do so at your peril. Those without debt get a spending boost.

Fourth: Create business opportunities from an investment in productive infrastructure at all scales, based on turning waste into food and adding value with what's available. Small and large scales co-exist, collaborate, and compete in new ways – a flourishing ecosystem of enterprise, using infrastructure to even the playing field. That's access to tools and resources like maker-labs, temporary materials storage, platform cooperatives (software), and low rent buildings and land.

The economy is a complex system. It is ever shifting. But what we know is it is these basic relationships – between the whole, the cycles, and the principles – feeding back over time, show us how the economy is doing. We can adjust these relationships, using the feedback we receive to better inform our future decision making.

Democracy and decision making

There is, of course, then the question of who decides and that is where a democratic society and its people come in. People must be active within the system to be part of the decision-making feedback cycle. Not once every four years active either. Citizens, business, and enterprise of all kinds lead a circular economy within the 'rules of the game'. These 'rules' are decided by an active citizenship, at all scales, in a flourishing democracy.

It is collaborative networks of socially engaged people that energise and make productive and effective systems possible. Digital technologies can advance participation in communities, health, entrepreneurship, business, politics, and democracy – enriching feedback loops to better inform our decisions. But be warned, digital's shadow is dark and long. Digital can be used to enclose and enslave the system – making change more difficult and anti-democratic.

This is not easy. Nothing worthwhile ever is but we believe our approach frames a set of important and mutually reinforcing relationships. It is their feedback, over time, that holds the key to shifting an economy – from one that degenerates capitals and democracy, in a self-defeating slide into wealth extraction and extinction, towards a thriving, circular, new normal.

A circular economy, in essence, is a shift from the *extraction* to the *circulation* of the productive, materials, cycle and the gatekept, asset-based, cycle simultaneously. From degenerating capitals to regenerating and restoring. These cycles are symbiotic and nested within our living planet. A circular economy is, therefore, best thought about from a living systems perspective.

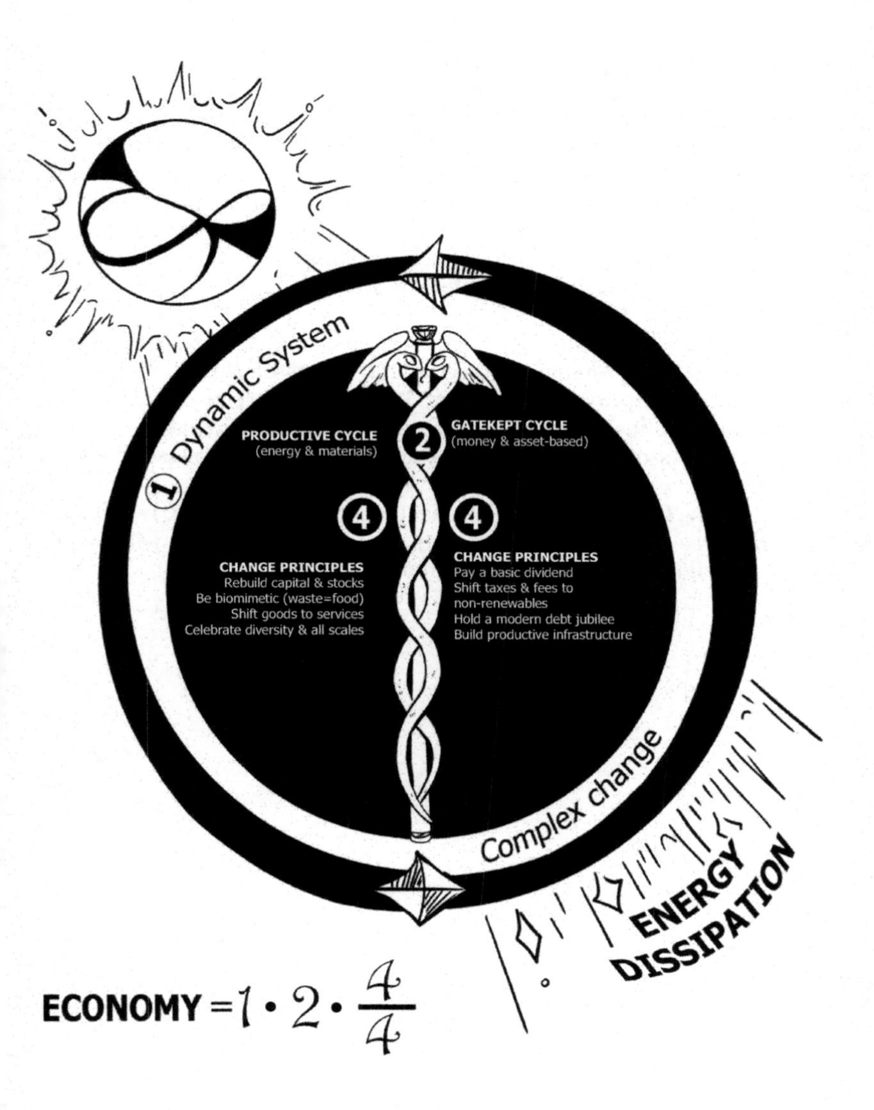

$$\text{ECONOMY} = 1 \cdot 2 \cdot \frac{4}{4}$$

References

Hanauer, N. and Beinhocker, E. (2014). Capitalism Redefined; What Prosperity Is, Where Growth Comes From, Why Markets Work, and How We Resolve the Tension between a Prosperous World and a Moral One. *Democracy: A Journal of Ideas, 31*. Cited in M. Bucganan (2014, April 02). *Why We Misunderstand Capitalism*. [online]. Available at https://medium.com/the-physics-of-finance/why-we-misunderstand-capitalism-2f606f111cf5 [Last accessed 09 May 2021].

Turner, A. (2017). *Between Debt and the Devil: Money, Credit, and Fixing Global Finance*. Princeton, NJ: Princeton University Press.

Webster, K. (2016). Metaphors of Prosperity (Part 1). *Circulate*. 16 March. [online]. Available at https://medium.com/circulatenews/the-metaphors-of-prosperity-part-1-e9cc309b9a86 [Last accessed 09 May 2021].

Wikipedia. (2021, April 04). Gatekeeping (communication). *Wikipedia the Free Encyclopaedia*. [online]. Available at https://en.wikipedia.org/wiki/Gatekeeping_(communication).

17 Today's economic narrative

Before we can begin to reimagine, we must first get closer to our economic narrative as imagined now.

Physicists impressed the economists of the 19th and early 20th centuries. These economists went in search of parallel laws of economic relationships to those in physics. If they could find them, then economics would be the queen of social science. If the physicists could drill down to fundamentals and use this analysis to understand, predict, and control, then why not apply a mechanistic lens to economics?

The economy, in an era of machines, is a specific machine. It is one where the individual firm, worker or consumer is a rational, separate actor who chases maximum satisfaction and accepts the discipline of the market, since it gives the most efficient result possible. When aggregated, individual decisions can describe an Economy. Big E.

The metaphor then switches slightly to an Economy as engineered pipework. In the pipes is money. Money represents production and consumption exchanges, with prices acting as messages.

Here is a familiar diagram, based on Paul Samuelson's best-selling 20th century book *Economics* (e.g., Samuelson, 1948; Samuelson and Nordhaus, 2009).

This pipework is a stylised closed loop of money in exchange. Money is representing stuff – goods and services. It is, unsurprisingly for engineering pipework, all valves and no leaks. Via the market (the interaction of supply and demand), there is

DOI: 10.4324/9781003217657-20

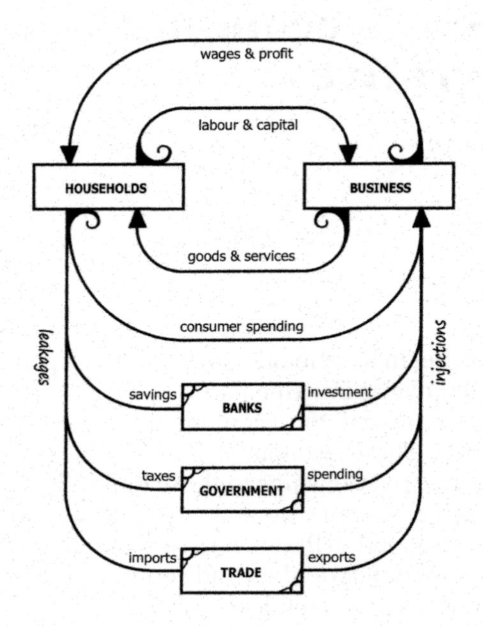

An economy as engineered pipework. After Samuelson.

equilibrium in the long run. It must work this way, it is pipework! There is nothing creative or indeterminate about it.

This pipework metaphor represents the entire Economy, with money fixed and also seen as a kind of lubricating oil in the machine of exchange. All will be well if people fit the machine, which must stay equalised to be efficient. That is why we have governments balancing budgets and exchange rates balancing trade. The Economy is like the pipework of a central heating system. It is a closed system that requires balance for the water within it to flow and heat efficiently.

If our current imagined economic narrative stopped there, perhaps all would be well but it doesn't. It goes on to suggest that it can produce growth from within. This closed system of pipework can produce more over time – through technology and innovation. Well, there are limits to the use of analogies. What is more, the narrative fails to say anything about what sits beyond the pipework; the energy to drive it, the natural environment it depends on, and society, which gives it purpose.

It is a picture of utopia with disappointment seemingly waiting at the corner. But it is a metaphor, a simplifying of reality. It can't do everything, right? But does it do enough? Clearly, it fulfils Harari's criteria for social change as it is a narrative about human motivation and how the future can be better. But evidence on the ground today, particularly in the wreckage of the Coronavirus downturn, suggests that this narrative is both broken and inadequate.

To find a starting point for the idea of an economy that resonates with the needs of these times, we must abandon the 'engineered pipework' image. We must replace it with something more contemporary and realistic.

To do that, we are going back in history for, as the last Queen of France, Marie Antoinette, somewhat perceptively is believed to have said: "There is nothing new except what has been forgotten".

For just as we uncovered with *The Wonderful Wizard of Oz*, by looking back we might rediscover great, long-forgotten ideas to help an alternative narrative emerge.

And so, we look back to before mechanical science, to the archetype of the regenerative process, and work forward from there. In The Imaginary that follows, a series of insights take us back to the pre-science circularity archetype, move through its curious lessening in today's mechanical economic story, and into real-world regenerative systems – revealed thanks to contemporary science and insights from living systems.

The remainder of this book then details our journey, or our 'yellow brick road' if you like, through history to arrive at insights that, when blended become mutually reinforcing. They offer the basis for an alternate narrative structure – a contribution to a new economic story offering both resonance and hope.

References

Samuelson, P. A. (1948). *Economics: An Introductory Analysis, 1st edition*. London: McGraw-Hill.
Samuelson, P. A. and Nordhaus, W. D. (2009). *Economics: An Introductory Analysis, 19th edition*. London: McGraw-Hill Education.

18 Worldview pre-science

Our journey starts in the 16th century, before the Age of Enlightenment. It is a world view ordained, ordered, and animated by God. Humanity's role was to draw closer to God by understanding and participating in the mystery with the guidance of the Church. It was an encompassing sort of order and in a strange way quite iterative. Knowledge was handed down. One of these traditions (not exactly Church approved), was alchemy – the transformation of materials. They too could surely be perfected in a sacred world, and in more refined traditions this process, or effort, transformed the alchemist too.

It was no mere pastime. In an era when printing was expensive, more than 4,600 publications on alchemy are known to originate between 1470 (and the early printing press) and the 18th century (and the rise of modern science) (McLean, 1996).

Alchemy was a pervasive and powerful narrative. Almost like discussing economics, Alchemy is highly symbolic and deemed practical only for the adept. Allegory and symbolism were often also used to communicate its complex philosophical beliefs.

This alchemical dragon-snake illustration, first used around 1600 BC, shows a beast endlessly eating its tail to stay alive. It transforms and continues forever.

The dragon-snake symbolises a story doing two things. It is trying to grasp the whole, and to imagine the system at work – the process. It points to the infinite cycle of nature's creation and destruction, life and death. Complementary opposites help express this idea. The perfection of the human, and all things, comes then through cycles – dissolution and coming together.

DOI: 10.4324/9781003217657-21

Constant recreation and transformation, through iteration. Behind is the Tree of Life.

Alchemy then suggests something important about a circular process even if set within a utopia. That while we strive for perfection, the *process* of repeatedly and iteratively trying to achieve it is valuable – perhaps more so than the outcome. As the late photojournalist, artist, and activist, Dan Eldon, captured in his work and is the title of a book about it: "The journey is the destination" (Eldon, 2011).

For many, the idea of making gold from lead was the purpose of Alchemy, rather than it also being the tool for a greater purpose – the perfection of self or enlightenment or a reflection on the necessity of being in tune with the sacred. These failed experiments around furnaces and flasks did manage to create some of the foundations for modern chemistry however, so never dismiss unintended consequences!

Something like this narrowness of vision exists today about the economy. The prevalent view is that it is an end not a means – seen as a linear process that turns everything into today's gold... money.

But this misses the wider value that is inbuilt into the process. Where is the Tree of Life, for example? We are imagining an economic process that mirrors, symbolically at least, the inbuilt value in Alchemy – bettering everything that participates in its process, to be regenerative of the whole system.

Our current but limited 'ends' view also skews how we see the elements of which the economy comprises.

In Alchemy, four, known, traditional elements 'earth, air, fire and water' represent matter. These are animated by a fifth element: The life force, known as the quintessence, which is symbolised by the dragon-snake.

If then energy, materials, money (as a medium of exchange) and the commons (endowed resources) are collectively the *imagine*d four elements of our stylised understanding of the economy, then the fifth element is missing; there is no quintessence – no life force.

If we momentarily cycle forward to the 20th century, to the economist, Kenneth Boulding, a prolific, forward-thinking writer, we are reminded that an economy consists of 'knowledge, materials and energy'. Knowledge then, because of the way it 'in-forms' gives meaning and structure to matter. Knowledge is our economy's hidden fifth element, or at least part of it. And the codeword for knowledge today? Technology.

The fifth element is critical because, just as in Alchemy, there is an exchange between the different material elements in the process of the economy. After many cycles, working through an animating fifth element, there is the potential for a changed form. By understanding what our economy's animating fifth element is, there is the potential for change – for us that change is to become a regenerative economic system.

In addition to a conventional view of technology, there is something else intrinsically linked to knowledge. It too animates the system – it is the social technology of money as credit. It may not be immediately obvious because money has two roles within today's economic system – it is both passive and active.

We are most familiar with money's passive role, as a medium of exchange. In a textbook, an economy is seemingly about barter between producers and consumers. That exchange, facilitated by money, means money acts like oil in a machine. Money in its exchange role (and as a temporary store of value (savings) to allow further investment in production), serves as a means – simply a way of getting around barter to facilitate production and consumption.

But money has a second active role that many do not see. It *animates* the system. Money, as credit, is often created from nothing – and even from the days when gold was a standard, it was still given a value way above what it cost to mine by the stamp upon it (and it was the security for lending promissory notes). Money is not a fixed commodity; it is not a given. It is more akin to knowledge, a promise to pay or, as British economist, Ann Pettifor (2017), names it "a social construct". Money is an agreement, with a purpose – a share in a better life, a call on the future. Just like Alchemy's dragon-snake, it is the quintessence, both active and activating – more like rocket fuel than engine oil.

We can't usefully discuss the potential for a regenerative economy by staying within the four, currently imagined, elements of our economy – energy, materials, money (in its passive role) and the commons (land and other endowed resources). We must reimagine our economy, animated by the fifth element... knowledge: technology and money in its active role as credit. The dragon-snake must eat its tail but instead, today's dragon-snake captures and guards the treasure – serving as a gatekeeper.

To recap. What we have is an economy, seen as a machine, operating in isolation – failing to grasp its part of a larger whole, a machine for processing all resources and converting all capitals (natural, social, and human) towards an end goal of ever greater financial capital. This engineered, throughput, rocket-fuel powered machine doesn't take account of the energy needed to drive it, the environment it depends upon, and the society that gives it purpose. Financial capital stands for all capitals, supposedly substituting natural, social, and human capitals, if the price is right. Consequently, the useful technology of money as credit, designed to bring forward production, increasingly fails to close the loop – it is not widely recirculated but adds to the 'treasure' such as stocks, bonds, derivative options, and real estate values.

Rather than being creatively 'alchemical' then, our economy is the opposite, it is now extractive and degenerative. It is harming not helping many of the participants involved in its process. Our inability to see all the elements our economy comprises, and their real role within it, clouds our understanding

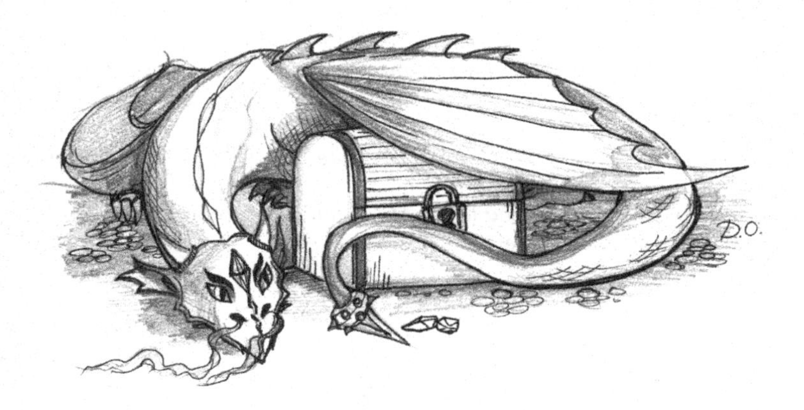

of what our economy does. It's why we find it difficult to comprehend the disconnect between our economy's promise and the reality it delivers.

While Alchemy would fade to give way to the Enlightenment (the Age of Reason in the 17th and 18th centuries), it perhaps offers us golden, yet forgotten, insights like:

- To achieve transformation, we need ongoing, circular, iterative processes and these are nothing new.
- There's inbuilt value in a 'good process' as a means, not an end.
- There's interdependence of the process within a wider system 'in service to life' (Lovins et al., 2018).
- A narrative being crucial to engagement, even if it has never led to heaven.

If the economy's purpose then is an enduring, dynamic set of relationships in service to life, it suggests that, just like alchemy, an economy needs a meaning outside itself because it is narrative, rather than gold, that ultimately draws us on.

References

Eldon, K. (2011). *Journey Is the Destination: Journals of Dan Eldon.* San Francisco, CA: Chronicle Books.

Lovins, L. H., Wallis, S., Wukman, A. and Fullerton, J. (2018). *A Finer Future: Creating an Economy in Service to Life: A Report to the Club of Rome.* Gabriola Island and British Columbia: New Society Publishers.

McLean, A. (1996). *The Alchemy Website.* Internet. www.alchemy-website.com

Pettifor, A. (2017). *The Production of Money: How to Break the Power of Bankers.* London: Verso.

19 Shifting the metaphor

From machine to metabolism

If not a machine or pipework as a metaphor to think about the economy, then what?

The machine metaphor is so simple. It connects input and output. There is a direct correlation. It is a linear relationship – I pull the handle I get the result. But if output and input are no longer related in the obvious way, then we need a metaphor that is non-linear, something dependent on connection.

Rather than machine, perhaps our new economic metaphor is more metabolic? Like an organism or even an organism in the context of its ecosystem.

But ecosystems are living systems, and these are complicated, complex, and diverse. They are full of feedback, from inside and out. Living systems evolve and change. That makes them harder to visualise. So, to make it more tangible, here we compare two complex systems with circulation – blood and money. In fact, comparing these circulations goes back to the time of the first economists we might recognise – de Qwesnay and the Physiocrats in the 18th century (Monroe, 1923).

Insight from living systems

Money within the economy is like blood in a living creature. Blood must reach every cell for the body to survive. It does so by flowing through large, medium, and small channels. Its boundary is not just the obvious pipework (arteries and veins) but thousands of miles of capillaries, just wide enough for single

DOI: 10.4324/9781003217657-22

blood cells. Indeed, 80% of the miles of blood vessels are capillaries. The cells of the body are one boundary and the body itself then connects to sources of input (food) and output (waste). Importantly, the blood system nests within the body's other systems. But the body itself sits within a wider ecosystem and its waste becomes food for that bigger system.

Insight from the Roman god Janus

So, the first insight about complex living systems is that they are Janus-faced. Named after the Roman god of 'beginnings,

gates, transitions, time, duality, doorways, passages, and endings,' Janus faced the past and the future. Let's also imagine he viewed the smaller and the larger system simultaneously. Arthur Koestler (1983) used this idea in his book *Janus*. It is one of the first broadly based books linking complexity with philosophy. For him, this way of organising was a *holarchy*, nested systems where whole and part have a mutual relationship.

The money circuit of an economy needs to work like the blood system – effectively reaching everywhere in a nourishing way. An *effective* system is more than an *efficient* one. Effectiveness is about the whole system and its purpose. Efficiency by contrast, just means a relationship between input and output. It has no purpose in a systems sense. Our current emphasis in simplified descriptions is usually on efficiency. If we cannot sense the periphery, then we tend to ignore it.

Consider the blood flow in this illustration.

The temptation is just to notice the big channels (arteries and veins) and the pump (heart). Yet, much action takes place at the periphery – at the level of the tiny capillaries and individual cells. The work happens at a myriad of exchanges. We must look at exchanges, not only flow functions.

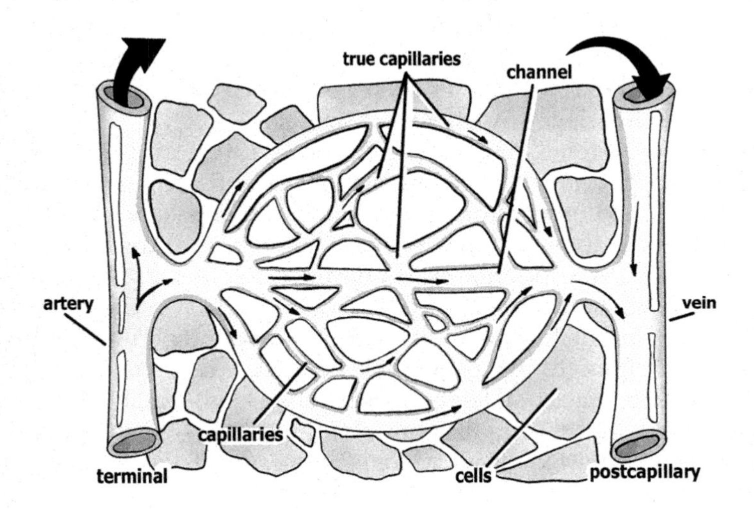

The contemporary world obsesses with efficiency. This is really a throughput or flow idea about getting more from less.

"The linear economy is driven by the bigger-better-faster-safer syndrome," says one of the circular industrial economy's founding fathers, Walter Stahel (e.g., Stahel, 2016).

In a linear economy of machine thinking, the parts are the focus and whether they work well. "Well," is determined by specific performance targets, for example, how inputs are related to outputs. The whole then is just the sum of the parts.

But in complex systems, like those of blood and money, the emphasis is on the relationships within a nested system. It is much more than individual parts; the focus is effectiveness. And, 'effectiveness is efficiency plus redundancy over time'.

In an aeroplane, there are redundant systems, their use intended only for when a main system fails. Air masks, for example, only become available when the cabin pressure system fails, yet no one complains about this 'hardly used' equipment as inefficiency.

In blood circulation, damage to parts of the system, say bruising or bleeding, is not usually fatal. Blood flow is flexible, the body can heal, and there is spare capacity for coping. Capillaries can shut off, blood rerouted. There is *redundancy* built into the system. There is resilience brought about by the many small pathways, nodes, and an ability to self-repair. By contrast, when an efficient 'big flow' pipe in a very efficient system fails, it is often fatal. Efficiency can mean brittleness.

Effective systems, unlike efficient ones, reveal an interplay between large and small; delivery/recovery and exchange; and the system and its environment. This is why anyone who only wants to talk about efficiency is missing what makes such a complex system work; they are assuming the contexts. This can be a fatal one-sidedness.

Here is a test of it: 'It's a great business idea now try running it in Somalia'. It might well be possible but *assuming* benign business contexts – accessible public institutions, enforceable legal contracts, working infrastructure, banking, etc. – is a flawed approach when we know all systems are nested. There are subsystems and there are systems which enfold our system.

'We talk about the forest as well as the trees,' explains Cradle to Cradle pioneer, Michael Braungart (McDonough and Braungart, 2002). It is odd that he must repeatedly make the point since the trees, shrubs, and other life are obviously nested within a forest ecosystem. And yet the point remains largely ignored. Braungart uses the idea, popularised by management 'guru', Peter Drucker, that there is a difference between "doing the right thing and doing things right". The former suggests understanding effectiveness and the latter just efficiency – important as it is.

What makes an effective system?

Sally Goerner et al. (Fullerton, 2015) helped illustrate what makes an effective system in this graphic. It could be related to blood, oxygen, money, or energy systems.

The outcome for an enduring, adaptable, effective system is the *interplay between efficiency and resilience.*

Effectiveness is a system design, or intention, in the real world of change and complex systems aimed at enduring. Go too much towards efficiency and brittleness follows. Go too far towards resilience and change becomes difficult – the system unresponsive, dying even.

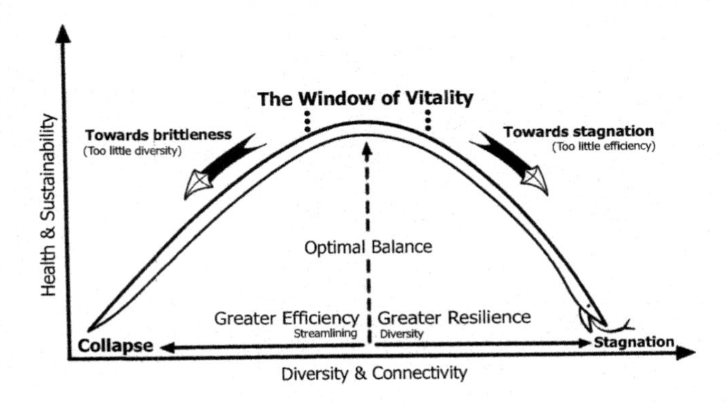

The window of vitality. Adapted from Sally Goerner, Bernard Lietaer, Bob Ulanowicz (Ulanowicz et al., 2009).

Insight from the Greek god Pan

Over time, these dynamic living systems grow, develop, break-down, and reorder with strong recognisable patterns. Buzz Holling, the Canadian ecologist, calls this 'panarchy', which tries to explain the interplay in systems between change and persistence, between the predictable and unpredictable (Resilience Alliance, n.d.).

This time the calling is of the Greek god of nature, Pan, whose persona also gave an image of unpredictable change, strength, and energy so we can also consider dynamic living systems as Pan-like.

The Greek god of nature, Pan.

Panarchy helps us understand how all kinds of complex systems (including ecological, social, and economic), evolve and adapt. Thomas Homer-Dixon (2010) has observed how panarchy shares similarities with other theories about adaptation and change in complex dynamic systems. His core idea is that systems naturally grow, become brittle, collapse, and then renew themselves in an endless cycle. This notion recurs repeatedly in literature, philosophy, religion, and studies of human history, as well as in the natural and social sciences.

But Holling does more than simply restate this old idea. Through his impressive theoretical research, he has made it more precise, powerful, and practical. He does so by distinguishing between potential, connectivity, and resilience. He identifies variations in a system's pace of change as it moves through its cycle and describes the roles of adjacent cycles in the grand hierarchy of cycles.

So be it a healthy blood or money system, a kind of 'circularity' prevails. Within it are adaptive cycles and feedback creating dynamic stability. Surplus energy powers these cycles. In the real world, the surplus powering our living system is energy from the sun.

Every economy is a monetary economy as well as a materials, products, and services economy. The creation and use of money as credit gives money a more active role. Added to knowledge,

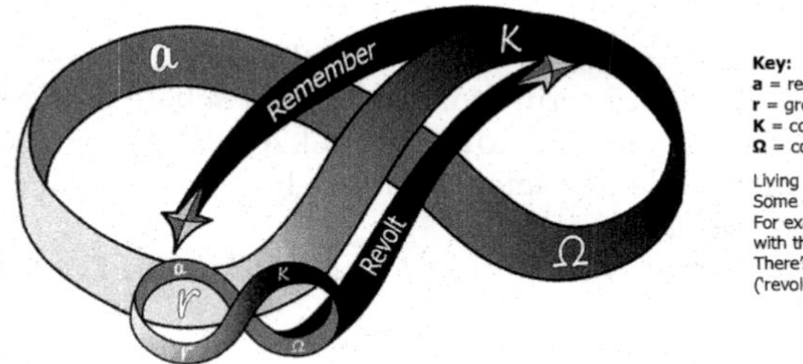

Key:
a = reorganisation
r = growth
K = conservation / maturity
Ω = collapse release of nutrients

Living systems nest within each other. Some cycles move faster than others. For example, a tree compared with the whole forest. There's an interplay between change ('revolt') and resilience ('remember').

Remember & revolt. After Holling.

it intertwines with energy surplus as a means of creating economic growth.

In summary, effective, purpose-orientated systems are characterised by the interplay between:

- Efficiency and resilience – the twin functions we characterise as a bias to 'structure/flow' (for efficiency) and then 'network/exchange' (for resilience)
- Being Janus-faced – nested
- Panarchy – which shows the relationship between 'remember' and 'revolt' across nested systems. This is both creative and destructive by turns. No system endures forever or remains unchanged, and
- An energy surplus being available.

What different perspective interdependent, non-linear systems bring. There is one process in the economy, but it is not machine-like, it is far more dynamic, interdependent, and feedback rich; it has therefore 'circularity'.

References

Fullerton, J. (2015). *Regenerative Capitalism. How Universal Principles and Patterns Will Shape Our New Economy.* [online]. Available at http://capitalinstitute.org/wp-content/uploads/2015/04/2015-Regenerative-Capitalism-4-20-15-final.pdf [Last accessed 10 May 2021].

Homer-Dixon, T. (2010). Complexity Science and Public Policy. Articled based on the Manion Lecture for the Canada School of Public Service, Ottawa, Canada, 05 May 2010. [online]. Available at https://homerdixon.com/complexity-science-and-public-policy-speech/ [Last accessed 10 May 2021].

Koestler, A. (1983). *Janus: A Summing Up, New Edition.* London: Picador.

McDonough, W. and Braungart, M. (2002). *Buildings Like Trees, Cities Like Forests.* London: The Catalog of the Future, Pearson Press. [online]. Available at https://mcdonough.com/writings/buildings-like-trees-cities-like-forests/ [Last accessed 10 May 2021].

Monroe, A. E. (1923). *Early Economic Thought: Selections from Economic Literature Prior to Adam Smith,* pp. 336–348. Cambridge, MA: Harvard University Press.

Resilience Alliance (n.d.). Panarchy [online]. Available at https://www.resalliance.org/panarchy [Last accessed 10 May 2021]. Originally in L. H. Gunderson and C.S. Holling (2002). *Panarchy: Understanding Transformations in Human and Natural Systems*. Washington, DC: Island Press.

Stahel, W. R. (2016, March 23). The Circular Economy. *Nature: International Weekly Journal of Science, 531*(7595). [online]. Available at https://www.nature.com/news/the-circular-economy-1.19594#:~:text=The%20linear%20economy%20is%20driven,of%20cheap%20and%20sexy%20goods [Last accessed 10 May 2021].

Ulanowicz, E. R., Goerner, S., Lietaer, B. and Gomez, R. (2009). Quantifying Sustainability: Resilience, Efficiency and the Return of Information Theory. *Ecological Complexity, 6*(1), 27–36. doi:10.1016/j.ecocom.2008.10.005

20 The productive cycle

Four rules for materials to flow not fail our economy

The textbook economy is an idealised economy of production, consumption, and exchange – powered by fossil fuels. It is barter, with a veil of money. It is about products, components, and materials but ignores resource stocks and waste sinks.

In the real world, we need space and time to transition to renewables and to cope with the decline in the quality and availability of metals and minerals. Rethinking production, exchange, and the notion of waste, as well as rebuilding eroded natural capital might give us that.

In the 1990s, numerous books made the case for a modern economy, with sophisticated materials flows and better product, service, and system design. *Natural Capitalism* originally published in 1999 was, perhaps, the best of these (Hawken et al., 1999, 2009).

It looks beyond flows, exploring how to improve stocks, especially natural capital.

> ...natural capital, on which civilization depends to create economic prosperity, is rapidly declining, and the rate of loss is increasingly proportionate to gains in material well-being.
>
> Amory and Hunter Lovins with Paul Hawken, *Natural Capitalism* (1999, P11)

Natural capital encompasses all earth's resources and living systems. It includes water, minerals, oil, trees, fish, soil, air,

DOI: 10.4324/9781003217657-23

grasslands, savannas, wetlands, estuaries, oceans, coral reefs, riparian corridors, tundras, and rainforests. The book's authors talk about four essential shifts to reverse natural capital's decline. Two decades on they remain essential:

1. Radical resource efficiency
2. A shift from goods to services
3. Be bio-mimetic so that waste = food
4. Rebuild natural capital

Around the same time as the publication of *Natural Capitalism*, Bill McDonough and Michael Braungart (2002) were writing *Cradle to Cradle*. They posed the question: How could we remake the way we make things? They identified three main principles for switching to a net-positive production model – one mimicking nature's regeneration cycle:

1. Celebrate diversity
2. Shift to renewables/clean energy
3. Waste = food

We've reordered their list to start with 'celebrating diversity' as the pointer towards systems thinking. For in a complex, adaptive system, diversity is strength, a source of creativity, and resilience. We follow diversity from their list with the desperately needed energy shift, before finally listing their materials question – where the important principle is 'waste = food'. Today, McDonough and Braungart talk increasingly of a 'nutrient economy'.

Implied within 'rebuilding natural capital' is the 'waste = food' equation. The 'forest feeds the trees'. The forest, its soils, the fallen and living plant matter, is a stock made from converted solar energy. That stock is also a source of nutritious flows. It is a virtuous cycle. Everything within a forest serves a purpose, not by design but through evolution: it is the survival of the 'fitting-most'. It is a complex and interconnected ecosystem, with each element positively reinforcing the whole with elements of competition and cooperation entwined. A forest wastes nothing – except energy. Energy flows through and everything is food, fuelling the forest's growth. It is the collective that determines a forest's ability to thrive.

When discussing waste = food with organic matter (like that of a forest), the equation seems logical, almost straight-forward. The forest analogy makes sense. But how does it work if someone runs through the forest contaminating it – say by dropping a plastic bottle and leaving it on the forest floor?

McDonough and Braungart identify two types of materials: Biological (natural/organic) and technical (manufactured). The key to 'waste = food' is separating biological and technical materials by keeping each in their own cycle.

To understand which cycle something sits in simply ask, 'where is order rebuilt?' If only humans can restore order, it is technical and should not enter the biosphere.

In the biosphere are products of consumption. In other words, products that get 'used-up' (think tomatoes). In the technosphere are products of service. We 'use' these products but they are not 'used-up' (think smartphones). This offers valuable insight. In a circular economy, you need both regenerative and restorative approaches to enable the 'waste = food' principle to rebuild natural and manufactured capitals, respectively.

This diagram is based on *Cradle to Cradle* design protocol. It shows the two material cycles and is 'regenerative and restorative by intention and design'.

The basic stories of *Natural Capitalism* and *Cradle to Cradle* interweave nicely and, in 2009 following the second of this century's three financial crashes so far, others began to strengthen and reframe their work. Organisations such as the Ellen MacArthur Foundation shaped a bigger picture sense of the business and conventional economic case for a 'circular economy'.

For many, a circular materials economy is inevitable. Without it, the aspirations of several billion world citizens will only accelerate our resources overshoot and climate breakdown (EMF, 2019). The challenges are enormous from an energy,

Biological and technical material cycles. Adapted from Webster and Johnson (2009).

resources, and systems perspective. *Cradle to Cradle* asks that we 'celebrate diversity'. *Natural Capitalism* asks that we do 'whole system design'. But we don't, still widely ignoring or misunderstanding both.

Instead, much of today's circular economy discussions are bogged down in waste management, the need for a renewable energy surplus and resource efficiency in materials production at large scales. What is missing is the need to:

- Address stock maintenance not just flows. Flows are active so attract our attention, but stocks are rebuilt or depleted over time by flows. That matters because as the age old saying goes: 'You can't draw water from a dry well'.

- Be regenerative. We must find ways to rebuild rather than deplete the natural and social capitals upon which our continued productivity depends.
- Consider all scales. We need structures that combine efficient channels and effective exchange at the small and medium scale – as well as the large.

Given this, as circular thinking for the productive cycle enters its third decade, in its contemporary guise, we suggest four updated rules:

1. Regenerate & restore all capitals
   - Think: Natural & social capitals
2. Be bio-mimetic
   - Think: Waste = food
3. Sell performance and service
   - Think: Shift from selling goods to services/performance (with nature supplying services every bit as much as materials)
4. Optimise the whole system
   - Think: Effective whole not only efficient parts (include all scales).

Yet, while these updated rules can help fix the mess that is our 'products economy', they will never, in isolation, lead to a full circular economy. For while we understand our products, components, and materials are in an intimate dance with the economy of natural and social capital, it is harder to see its intimate connection with money, debt, banks, and the extended realm of financial capital. And, that is not about the nuts and bolts of financing production and consumption. It is much more to do with how money is created and allocated and how that too circulates – or not. It is often about the ownership of assets and the economic rents others must pay to access them.

Some of our circular, regenerative economy is 'missing in action'. It is time to find it.

References

EMF. (2019). *Completing the Picture: How the Circular Economy Tackles Climate Change*. V.3–26 September 2019. Cowes, Isle of Wight: Ellen MacArthur Foundation. Available at https://www.ellenmacarthurfoundation.org/assets/downloads/Completing_The_Picture_How_The_Circular_Economy-_Tackles_Climate_Change_V3_26_September.pdf [Last accessed 10 May 2021].

Hawken, P., Lovins, A. and Lovins, H. (1999). *Natural Capitalism: Creating the Next Industrial Revolution*. New York: Little Brown & Company.

Hawken, P., Lovins, A. and Lovins, H. (2009). *Natural Capitalism: The Next Industrial Revolution (10th Anniversary Edition)*. Abingdon, Oxon: Earthscan/Routledge.

McDonough, W. and Braungart, M. (2002). *Cradle to Cradle. Remaking the Way We Make Things*. Berkeley, CA: North Point Press.

Webster, K. and Johnson, C. (2009). *Sense and Sustainability: Educating for a Low Carbon World*. Skipton: Terra Preta.

21 Uncovering the big players

Active but hidden in plain sight

An economy is always some combination of knowledge, materials, and energy. 'Knowledge' stands behind the very idea of civilisation and technology is one element. Money is also a technology if the definition of technology is science or knowledge put into practical use to solve problems or invent useful tools.

'Energy' stands for energy in surplus, cheap energy, and concentrated energy, whether from trees, from whales, or from the coal and oil of buried sunshine. We apply these energies to materials of all kinds – minerals, metals, forests.

To obtain a growing economy requires more than making and selling, it requires money. Perhaps that money is invested savings, but increasingly it is credit, newly created, to bring forward production. Cheap energy and cheap credit are a heady mix.

How credit creates economic growth and economic growth creates credit

Economic growth enables the repayment of the principal loan and interest. That gives confidence that new loans will also be serviced. Low or zero growth inhibits loans.

In a way, the owners of the money supply (the organisations behind the issuance of non-commodity fiat currency (governments) and those with banking licences), are creating, holding, and allocating useful, scarce, assets. Then, they are charging for access, for the use of them.

DOI: 10.4324/9781003217657-24

Finance: a big active player hidden in plain sight

In the power to create credit and decide where it is applied is a clue to why Finance is very 'active'. It shapes the economy.

When we say 'hidden' in the subtitle here, we mean a player beyond the familiar in our simplified, textbook, economic story – firms (producers), households (consumers), and government. Finance is not just an intermediary, matching savings with investment opportunities as the textbooks would have it.

So, might there be more hidden yet active big players?

In their powerful article, *'Finance Is Not the Economy'* Michael Hudson and Dirk Bezemer (2016) set out to describe who these players are and why our seeing them is so important to understanding the 'evolution and distribution of wealth and debt in today's global economy'.

Real estate and monopolies: big active players hidden in plain sight

Hudson and Bezemer (2016) identify two 'active' players, 'missing in action' from our simplified economic story. These are 'finance' (which we've already referred to above) and 'real estate and monopolies' (predominately land, property, and finite resource ownership, including copyright and patents).

Both these 'hidden' players share something in common – they can (and do) extract vast amounts of economic wealth. They do so by charging access fees. So, whether you want access to a bank loan or a privately-owned property – you will likely pay an access or use fee in the form of interest, admission or rent. In the world of economics, the access fees – that portion above what it actually takes to provide the service or access at a profit – are called 'economic rents'.

Economic rents are a surplus, but they aren't often competed away. That's because what the economic rent is raised against (be it land or copyright), is fixed or nearly fixed in supply. Scarcity pays.

Today's simplified economic story only focuses on 'earned income'. That is any money made that involves productively working for it. For most of us this is a salary in exchange for being a productive employee. Or a business that earns an income (profit) by converting materials and energy into new goods or services in a truly competitive marketplace.

What 'finance' and 'real estate and monopolies' both have in common is that they attract and extract a surplus, an 'unearned income'. It means those with these assets do not have to be productive in the traditional sense to make money, their 'business' is making returns by controlling access.

Michael Hudson describes it as a 'tollbooth' economy. And, the scarcer something is (like land for development with a coastal view or a specialist medicine), the higher the economic rents likely to accrue.

Taking Samuelson's textbook pipe diagram as a starting point, and synonymous with our simplified economic story, Hudson and Bezemer (2016) redraw the pipework, layer by layer, to provide a comprehensive and more accurate picture of our economy at work.

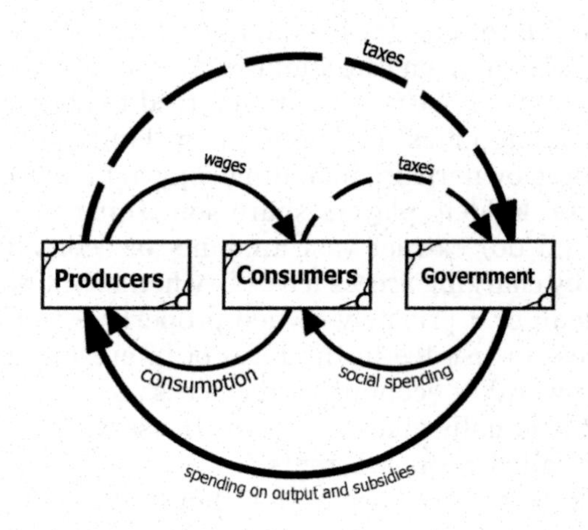

The traditional economy without a finance or trade sector. Adapted from Hudson and Bezemer (2016).

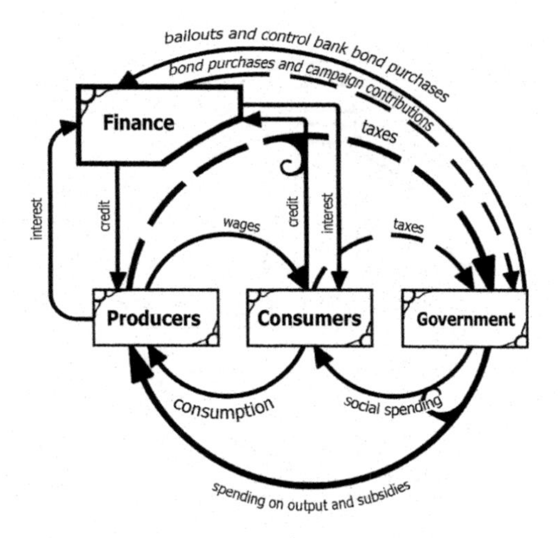

The traditional economy adding finance as an active player. Adapted from Hudson and Bezemer (2016).

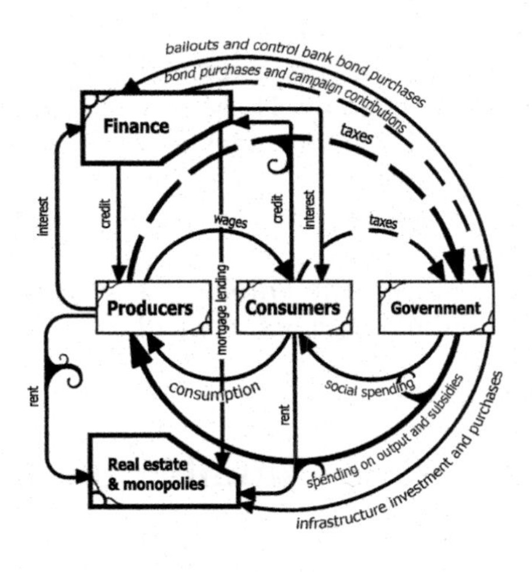

The traditional economy adding real estate as an active player. Adapted from Hudson and Bezemer (2016).

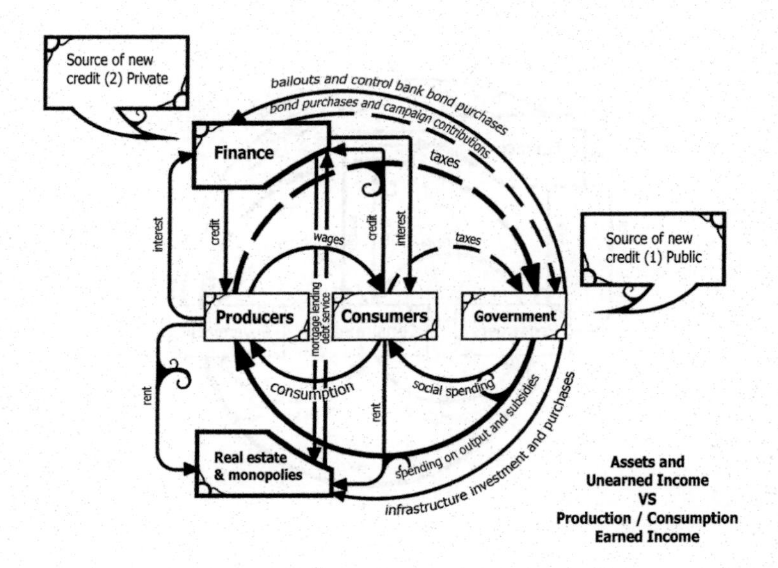

Identifying the places where new money is created. Adapted from Hudson and Bezemer (2016).

We know that money is not a fixed-supply commodity that shuffles around the economy. Those institutions with banking licences can create additional money from nothing, as can governments if they control the currency they use. In the last of the diagrams, Hudson and Bezemer are showing where additional money is created.

Mary Mellor (2010) in *The Future of Money* describes these places where additional money is created as two 'magic money trees':

Magic money tree – number one

Who creates this tree's additional money? The government. The government can supply as much money as it requires either from selling bonds or increasing national debt, which it never needs to pay off. It can just issue more debt – some of the UK's debts from 1720 were only redeemed in 2014 (Castle, 2014). Only the part held overseas is of real concern because large holdings abroad can reduce confidence in a country's own national currency. But a government does not have to borrow its own currency at all.

Where does it go? The government spends the additional money into existence (Mellor, 2010), then taxes it back to ensure stable prices.

This is 'our' magic money tree in a democratic society.

Magic money tree – number two

Who creates this tree's additional money? The banking sector. It does so by issuing loans, which are, in practice, not dependent on reserves or existing deposits. Banks create both the asset and the liability on their books. Why this is new money and why regulation for the UK's banking sector needs to change, is elegantly explained by Professor Richard Werner (2019) a banking and development economist in his interview '*Are banks good or bad?*' on *RT.com*.

In practice, this additional money is, overwhelmingly, loaned for existing assets like real estate, shares on the stock exchange, intellectual property and insurance.

How does this work through? Increased loans increase perceived value. Perceived increased value provides security for further loans and increases the attractiveness of the asset still further. This cycle increases confidence in the rest of the economy and some spending spills over to create additional growth. Owners of stocks receive dividends and, as for the housing market, the result is quite familiar.

An example: A landlord buys a property on a mortgage, lets it, and, in return, receives a monthly rent. The rent pays the landlord's monthly mortgage interest. Over the long-term, the value of the landlord's property is likely to increase; in practice, this is based on what a bank is willing to lend upon it. If nothing productive has happened, say property improvements, to create additional monetary value to the property, then the capital gain is an 'unearned surplus'.

> Landlords grow rich in their sleep without working, risking or economising.
>
> John Stuart Mill (1848)

But housing (or even land) is not the only secure asset with the ability to leverage credit. Any asset perceived as scarce and marketable can be the subject of asset inflation – examples include 'growth stocks' [shares without dividends] artworks, classic cars, fine wines, and precious metals. As Hudson and Bezemer (2016) point out, banking too earns economic rents, with 'interest' being what we pay to rent money.

The world's gifts and who benefits from them

There are many ways to achieve the outcomes we desire in our societies and all need the endowments of the world – its sun, land, atmosphere, water cycles, biodiversity, mineral deposits. To this, we could add the wisdom of past generations, the designs for machinery, accumulated knowledge and social data, products, or systems.

One way to view these worldly gifts (or assets) is as a source of common wealth, which is often referred to as 'the commons'. We mentioned these earlier but now explore the concept.

An alternative view is that the world's gifts only hold value if 'husbanded' correctly – done by privately enclosing them, with suitable compensation going to the owner for their prudent management.

The commons, its enclosure, and who reaps the various rewards is an ancient tussle, going back in England to before 1217 and is particularly important when it comes to land. All classical economists from Adam Smith to Karl Marx identified the question of economic rents as central to their work and focused on land and landlords as one of the barriers to wider prosperity. Land, for classical economists, was one of the three factors of production – along with labour and capital. Land is more-or-less fixed in supply – 'they aren't making more of it'. So, when land is treated as a shared common under shared management, rather than held privately or fully enclosed by the State, it makes a big difference to who gets the benefits. Land can be a source of surplus from crops and forestry, from by-products, as well as for the minerals beneath it. But, in an age of increasing population and the development of cities, especially from the 19th century onwards, land has had a value from location rather than its soil – making it rather special.

Henry George's footnote in history

It was journalist turned politician, Henry George, that put land ownership and the impact of economic rents in the spotlight once more in the industrial era.

George powerfully explored the social tension of the late 19th century in America, in his hugely popular 1879 book *Progress and Poverty* (see George, 2006). And, in today's language, it trended. It sold three million copies.

Labour economist and author, George Henry Soule Jr (1887–1970) describes Henry George as: "By far the most famous American economic writer, [and] ...author of a book which probably had a larger worldwide circulation than any other work on economics ever written." (Soule, 1955, p. 81).

George and his followers wanted some portion of unearned income as *the* source of revenue and relief: through a land value tax, rather than taxing enterprise or workers.

Although George's influence was widespread, ultimately, he failed.

An assault against George's land tax ideas, principally led by US economist JB Clarke saw land lumped together with other kinds of capital in economic theory. This muddied the economic picture

– surely it is all productive now, isn't it? And, while George's ideas extended long after his own death in 1897, land, and its unearned income, subsequently became almost invisible in the new neo-classical economics (Gaffney, 1994).

Combined at that time with the rise of labour organisation, wages, social welfare, and economic growth, which eased the conditions of the poor, George's ideas faded and, arguably today, are much forgotten. Even Marx (Marx-Engels Correspondence, 1881) saw George as a footnote to economic history.

But questions about natural capital, the land, and the commons began resurfacing in the 1960s, as part of the environmental and 'rights' movements. Questions about who owns and who benefits from the land and other original wealth sources, gifted by the earth or previous generations, began to re-emerge.

Today, growing inequality coupled with a stumbling, low growth, production economy, has rekindled curiosity about the difference between 'earned and unearned income'.

It seems inequality – largely a consequence of ownership and economic rents/unearned income from real estate, intellectual property, stocks and shares, and financial instruments – is a feature not a bug in the system. Perhaps there are learnings from Henry George's legacy that will live on yet?

Makers versus Takers

No one more simply sums up the difference between 'earned and unearned income' than Rana Foroohar (2017), in her beautifully titled book: *Makers and Takers*. In our words not hers, makers make money by productively working for it (earned) and takers take money via access fees to assets (unearned). Foroohar's critique of unearned income talks about 'rent seeking' and the 'return of the rentier'. It is a live issue.

To make sense of real-world stocks, flows, and feedback, we need to 'see' all the economy's major actors. Our current simplified economic story means we already understand the productive 'makers'. Now, it is time to focus on the 'takers' – those owners of fixed assets and enclosers of the commons.

A single economic process with two distinctive aspects

Let's circle back to the beginning of this chapter then and Hudson and Bezemer's (2016) final diagram. There is no arguing their picture is more complex than Samuelson's simplified pipework. But let's face it if pipework really were *that* simple, we'd never need a plumber.

What Hudson and Bezemer illustrate are two distinctive aspects within one economic process. In bold are the flows around the physical and other assets including the credit money system

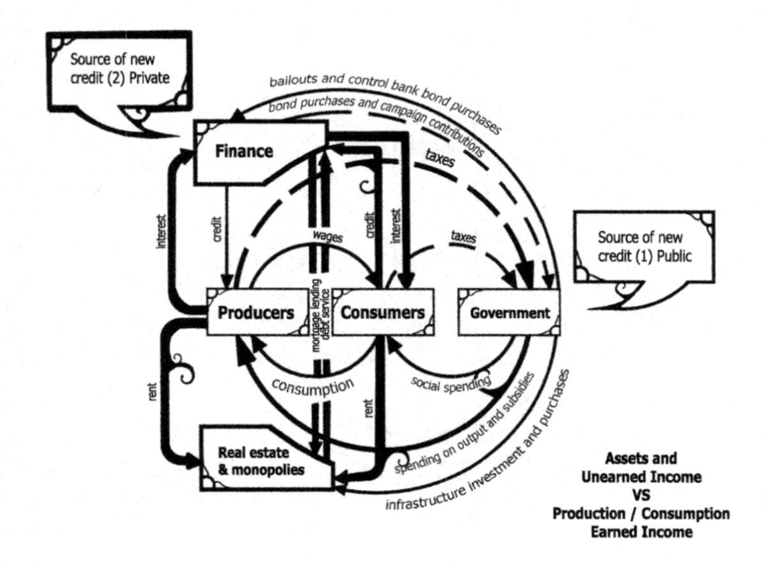

Full flows around the economy resulting from new sources of private credit. Adapted from Hudson and Bezemer (2016).

that attracts returns (economic rents) to their owners for allowing access.

In a thriving economy, money circulates. Importantly, it must circulate throughout the whole system – money, like blood, must reach the very periphery. But what tends to happen within the economy's second aspect (from unearned income takers) is that this money gets trapped – often stuck in an inflating, then bursting asset bubble. In short, it hurts and does not help the supporting economic system it is nested within. In Michael Hudson's view, it has become parasitical on the productive economy. Worse than this, it is an active preoccupation of governments across the globe to prop up asset values whenever a periodic crisis threatens them – as manifest in the trillions lavished in 2008 and 2020.

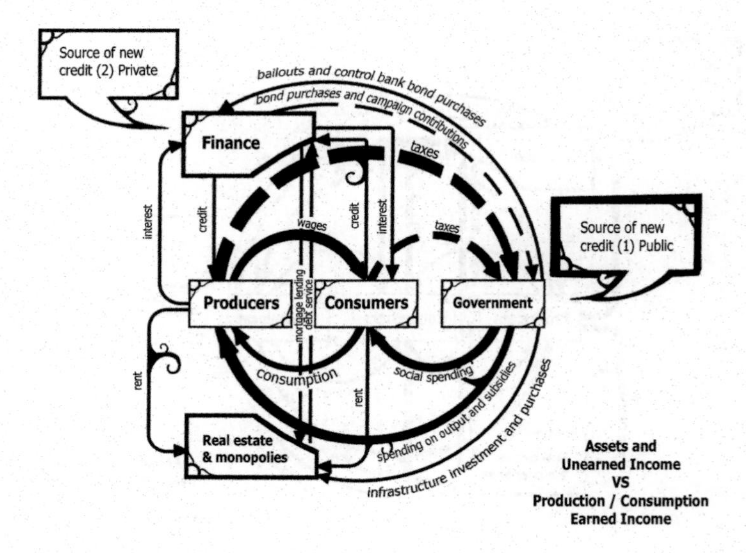

Full flows around the economy resulting from new sources of public credit. Adapted from Hudson and Bezemer (2016).

Healing the whole requires money to better circulate in the productive economy. The challenge is significant, and for some almost inconceivable. In an aside, and as ascribed to author Fredric Jameson: "It's easier to imagine an end to the world than an end to capitalism" (cited in Fisher, 2009).

So, just as we describe four rules for better circulation within a materials economy, next we offer four rules for better money retention and circulation within the productive cycle.

References

Castle, S. (2014). That Debt from 1720? Payment Is Coming. *The New York Times*. 27 December 2014. [online]. Available at https://www.nytimes.com/2014/12/28/world/that-debt-from-1720-britains-payment-is-coming.html [Last accessed 10 May 2021].

Fisher, M. (2009). *Capitalist Realism: Is There No Alternative?* Ropely, Hants: Zero Books.

Foroohar, R. (2017). *Makers and Takers: How Wall Street Destroyed Main Street*. New York: Crown Business.

Gaffney, M. (1994). Neo-Classical Economics as a Stratagem against Henry George. In M. Gaffney and F. Harrison (Eds.). *The Corruption of Economics*, pp. 29–164. London: Shepheard-Walwyn Publishing Co. Available at https://masongaffney.org/publications/K1Neo-classical_Stratagem.CV.pdf [Last accessed 10 May 2021].

George, H. (2006). *Progress and Poverty, New Edition*. New York: Schalkenbach (Robert) Foundation US.

Hudson, M. and Bezemer, D. (2016). Finance Is Not the Economy: Reviving the Conceptual Distinction. *Journal of Economic Issues*, *50*(3), 745–768. https://doi.org/10.1080/00213624.2016.1210384.

Marx-Engels Correspondence. (1881). *Marx to Friedrich Adolph Sorge in Hoboken*. Moscow: Progress Publishers. [online.] Available at www.marxists.org/archieve/marx/works/1881/letters/81_06_20 [Last accessed 26 June 2021].

Mellor, M. (2010). *The Future of Money: From Financial Crisis to Public Resource*. London: Pluto Press.

Mill, J. S. (1848). *Principles of Political Economy, with some of Their Applications to Social Philosophy: On the General Principles of Taxation, Book V, Chapter II*. New York: Appleton & Co. [online].

Available at https://www.econlib.org/library/Mill/mlP.html?chapter_num=67#book-reader [Last accessed 10 May 2021].

Soule, G. H. Jr. (1955). *Ideas of the Great Economists*. New York: Mentor.

Werner, R. (2019, March 27). Are Banks Good or Bad? On Financial sector problems and money creations. Interviewed on www.RT.com [online]. Available at https://www.youtube.com/watch?v=A49tHchSegg [Last accessed 10 May 2021].

22 The gatekept cycle

Four rules for money to circulate not clot our economy

> Almost all the strength of modern market economies is based on directing entrepreneurial activity from rent seeking into wealth creation.
>
> Economist, John Kay, *The Monumental Folly of Rent-Seeking* (2012)

Governments or banks can create money, but does it circulate or get stuck somewhere? If money is like blood and must reach everywhere, and continuously – the key is circulation. However, the velocity of money has been getting slower for years, that means the number of times a pound or dollar changes hands in a year has been falling. It is getting 'stuck' very quickly. If it were blood, we'd likely describe it as a blood clot.

The new money mostly gets lodged in assets, in the unproductive sector, which Michael Hudson nicely shorthands the FIRE (Finance, Insurance, and Real Estate) sector (Hudson and Bezemer, 2016). While our thinking reflects Hudson's, we're calling it the 'Gatekept cycle' because of the way so relatively few are guarding, access to and wealth generated from, these FIRE sectors. Some of the wealth generated in this cycle trickles down, a kind of wealth effect, but not much (Liberto, 2021). If money 'clots' when fed into the unproductive economy it follows that

DOI: 10.4324/9781003217657-25

to restore flow, we should be encouraging it towards productive infrastructure – rebuilding capital or capacity. That means:

- Injecting money into sectors that spend on designing and making goods and services, and the consumers and users who are buying them.
- Shrinking the preference for wealth accumulating assets over production and consumption, and the private debt overhang.
- Building the 'commons' – our natural and social capital, our broader resource base, including data.

To regenerate the shared infrastructure upon which we build a liveable world (including all markets), investment and where we direct it matters (Mazzucato, 2021).

Our collapsing income distribution system

"82% of all wealth created in the last year went to the top 1% [of the world's population], and nothing went to the bottom 50%," states Oxfam International's 2018 *'Reward work not wealth'* report (Pimentel et al., 2018). This signals the extent to which our money is failing to effectively circulate (and serve) the whole system. Money is 'clotting' so heavily in this gatekept cycle that our income distribution system is collapsing. That's because asset bubbles and ballooning debt extract (in mortgages, rent, healthcare, and interest payments), more of what income there is. Indeed, it is a 'trickle up' system.

We live in a world where for decades, the share of wages in developed-world national economies has stagnated or fallen. During that same time, the flexible yet precarious gig economy has grown rapidly (Azmanova, 2020). And, while AI and automation has been disruptive – its full impacts are hardly yet felt. Perhaps it is not surprising then that there is growing interest in an old, much written about, idea – some form of direct payment to citizens – often called a "basic income".

A limited example of this concept is the Alaska Permanent Fund. For business to extract some of Alaska's natural resources, like oil, fees are payable to a general fund distributed to citizens directly. It's a state-owned investment fund that's been paying an annual dividend to those living in Alaska since 1982. [https://apfc.org/].

Peter Barnes in his 2014 book '*With Liberty and Dividends for All*' explores how this concept could have application in America. Only a citizens' basic income is not really an 'income', as that makes it sound like something actively earned or perhaps given as welfare. The framing is important. Rather the concept is more akin to a *dividend or interest*. It is a share of the return from allowing others to exploit (by enclosing) those resources gifted by earth or left by previous generations. It is a citizen share of fees on enclosure, and it is a dividend.

For the purposes of illustrating the benefits, we are referring to it as a 'basic dividend'. It is encouraging to see others already thinking about its framing – like US 2020 Democratic presidential candidate, Andrew Yang, who calls it a 'freedom dividend' (Yang 2020). We also like the word 'interest' because of the multiple associations it affords – commUNITYinterest anyone? But we digress, we'll leave the naming and framing to experts like George Lakoff and focus on the underlying economic principle – the first of our four basic rules for money to better circulate in the productive economy.

All four rules are simply about 'circularity'. People must have the means (money, tools, and resources) to thrive, to participate freely in the economy – on their own terms. To have a reduced debt burden so they can spend on the goods and services they need and want. But how?

Rule 1: Distribute a basic dividend

The basic dividend is a key to ensuring citizens feel secure and have a share in what is the bounty of the earth, and what this generation has inherited. More pragmatically, from a purely economic perspective, it ensures there is enough demand for the goods and services produced in an era of easy overproduction and a fragmenting workforce (Roberts, 2010). This is not the old world, post-World War II, when employment was high and income taxes paid for welfare, when industry and commerce was national and there was a trade-off with labour.

The old 'capital versus labour' perception is primitive and out of sync with our times, just as 'market vs state' is. Contrastingly instead, earned and unearned stocks and flows are not only an interesting approach – a basic dividend is a practical and better fit for the world we are now in.

Long-time advocate and economist, Guy Standing, sets out five advantages. An interview by Deutsche Telekom (2017) with Standing sees him talk about why he supports a basic dividend/income. We paraphrase his reasoning here:

It is a social justice. 'The wealth and income of all of us has more to do with the efforts of our ancestors than anything we do for ourselves. If we allow private inheritance of wealth/influence/status, we should also have social inheritance. A basic income would be a sort of social dividend.'

It enhances freedom. "If I have basic income security, I have more freedom. The freedom to say no to an oppressive or abusive relationship or an exploitative employer. The freedom to go forth in society as an equal."

It provides a sense of security. And those who have security, says Standing, 'are more tolerant and altruistic. They have improved mental stability, IQ, and an improved capacity for long-term thinking. They tend to see themselves as citizens.'

It is a way of building a new income distribution system. 'Inequality is rising fast and won't come down through the traditional ways of raising wages. We won't see real wages on average rising much in OECD countries. Stagnation will continue if globalisation and the tech revolution continue, and a huge overhang of existing debt requires service. The basic dividend is a way of building a new distribution system. It is not an entire solution by itself, but it could help us prepare for the disruptive effects of robots and automation.'

It offers political stability. 'If we do not have a new system that gives people, ordinary people, basic income security, we'll see more and more political polarisation.'

There have been a variety of trials in different parts of the world experimenting with the notion of a basic dividend or income. They have usually resulted in a wealth of benefits well beyond the strictly economic. We touch on some of these in the fictional part of this book and offer some highlights here. The key though is not to look at the basic dividend, or any single idea, in isolation. Each forms one part of a solution in a complex system – how the parts influence one another within a wider whole is crucial to how we ultimately view their contribution and success.

- A reduction in bureaucracy. When everyone is eligible, a basic dividend is much easier and cheaper to administer than means testing state provided benefits. It is also much fairer.
- An increase in disposable income. People would have a guaranteed source of money to buy goods and services. In a flourishing productive economy, demand and supply hold equal importance.
- Greater entrepreneurship. Establishing any enterprise comes with risk but it is much easier to make the leap when there is a basic safety net. A basic dividend would be a catalyst for creativity and new jobs.

There are many evidence-based benefits, some more surprising than others. One trial in Canada saw hospitalization rates reduce by 8.5% – attributed to improved physical health. 'An increase in economic security reduced peoples stress, disease and self-destructive behaviour' (Cox, 2020).

> We are the wealthiest and most technologically advanced society in human history; it's time to invest in our people... Imagine your life and the lives of everyone you know with an extra $1,000 per month – how would you spend it? How would things change?
>
> Democratic presidential candidate, Andrew Yang, Yang2020.com

Rule 2: Shift taxes and fees

117,000 people lost their jobs in the UK's retail sector alone in 2018 according to the Centre for Retail Research. That figure rose to 143,000 in 2019 and, with the impact of coronavirus, 2020 was the worst for High Street job losses in more than 25 years with '200,000 job losses anticipated in the sector in 2021' (CRR, 2019; see also Nazir, 2019). Many blame the shift to online shopping. The political debate focuses on the unfair tax advantage online retailers have over their traditional counterparts. While it might be 'unfair' (most physical retailers reportedly pay double to eight times the tax rate of Amazon in the UK) (PYMNTS, 2019), this debate's focus, alongside others like it, consumes itself within the scope of existing taxes. This preoccupation distracts from bigger picture thinking about the logic of the tax system and how it fundamentally needs to change.

Today's assumption is that most taxes need to come from human labour (income taxes) and consumption (VAT or other sales taxes). An ever-decreasing amount comes from company profits or capital gains and little comes from the use of resources. But switching taxes from labour to pollution and resource use, could increase GDP, create more jobs and lower pollution according to research with the Ex'tax project – conducted in collaboration with organisations including Deloitte, EY, KPMG, PWC, Meijburg & Co, Trucost and Cambridge Econometrics (Groothuis, 2015).

A hundred years on and still the fossil fuel industry takes subsidies – either in production or by avoiding a contribution towards costs caused by their combustion (such as air pollution). Worldwide these subsidies total approximately $5 trillion – about the size of Japan's GDP [Figures calculated by the International Monetary Fund in their May 2019 working paper (Coady et al., 2019) and cited in Irfan (2019)]. Prices are messages but when subsidies are given, the 'true costs' are hidden – distorting prices and markets.

Times have changed, so too must our tax system.

A lengthy, though lesser reported, discussion is ongoing in certain circles about switching taxes from people and other renewables to non-renewables.

That might sound like just taxing fuel and mineral resources, or waste but the term *'non-renewables'* goes beyond that to include fixed assets which generate unearned income – from real estate, intellectual property, financial transactions, capital gains and data – which Clive Humby refers to as 'the new oil' (cited in Arthur, 2013).

What it is not, is a tax on profits from the productive economy – especially those reinvested. The shift is away from upping the costs of the productive economy and to penalising activity where unearned income or excessive economic rents are visible.

All the classical economists, from Adam Smith to Karl Marx, Henry George, and Thorstein Veblen, saw the taxation of economic rents as least likely to damage the economy. They saw it as a tax on surplus with an economic justice to it. Neo-classical economists disagreed. They saw any earnings in a market as justified because competition removes surplus in the long term. This then is an ancient debate indeed. In 1900, the ultimate non-renewable was land. The rationale for what was styled 'a natural resource tax' was made in just 50 words by Samuel Brazier writing in *The Public* (cited in LVT Fan's Blog, 2020).

> All men have equal right to life.
>
> Life depends absolutely upon land.
>
> Therefore all have equal right to land.
>
> Some must occupy more valuable land than others.
>
> Equal right demands that landholders pay the yearly value of land into a common fund for common purposes.

...Or they should at least pay for some of the resulting uplift.

This tax shift has a strong environmental rationale too as it promotes circulation and continued use of products, components, and materials – and disincentivises the extraction of new resources. Since these reuse and recovery activities are more labour intensive (because economies of scale are more limited), it can give another uplift to job opportunities.

One of the original thinkers who has continuously called for this tax shift is Founder-Director of the Product Life Institute in Geneva, Walter Stahel. He argues that:

> Exempting all renewable resources from taxation including work (human labour), and instead taxing the consumption of non-renewable resources and their undesirable polluting costs, creates a virtuous circle... It gives economic actors clear and powerful incentives to design more sustainable business models.
>
> (Stahel, 2011)

A positive systemic cycle in the economy then begins to emerge:

- A basic dividend provides security and autonomy, allows enterprise or small-scale working, and encourages demand for goods and services.
- A tax shift away from wages and production profits encourages the use of labour, investment, and entrepreneurship. Simultaneously, it discourages the use of raw materials and dampens the asset cycle.

It is about taking some of the unearned dividends (economic rents) from holding a scarce asset and giving it as one part of an 'unearned dividend' to everyone – although the implementation of a basic dividend does not depend on this tax. It could, for example, be spent into existence through the central bank in so called 'deficit spending' (Kelton, 2020). So, it is not a zero-sum game since it gives impetus to economic activity at the base and can increase prosperity over time – simply because the poor spend what they have and the rich do not spend all of it.

At the same time, it supports a circular materials economy – extending product life, cascading value, and closing the loop. It also stimulates the needed investment in infrastructure for this outcome to manifest – towards a renewables-based energy system and widespread regenerative agriculture. Indeed, the increasingly popular idea of a Green New Deal (Pettifor, 2019) meshes here seamlessly.

Rule 3: Arrange a debt jubilee

Making these stocks and flows of money work – circulate effectively – is not just about adding spending via a basic dividend as there is also the question of the existing debt burden. Debts take servicing. To avoid skewing figures, pre-pandemic borrowers in the UK were paying approximately £140 million *per day* in October 2019 in such debt service. This spending could be redirected of course but, as it stands, much of it feeds the financial system where it finds a new home in assets like real estate or stocks and shares (The Money Charity, 2019).

If asset bubbles hurt and do not help us, then we no longer want them to be the most salient feature our economies experience around the world. Neither do they have to be. It is possible to discourage investment in such bubbly assets by directing the criteria for the private creation of credit. Governments can issue 'guidance'. An early UK example was linking mortgages to a multiple of two to three times income maximum. Government can also direct its own spending and determine the rules for contracts.

'The *love* of money is the root of all evil,' so the old saying goes. In many ways, there is truth to this. Not money per se but a desire to accumulate rather than circulate it. This is the age-old tension – between money as a medium of exchange, essentially a tool, and money as a private store of value to be rented out.

Frederick Soddy, a Nobel winning scientist and ardent economic researcher, phrased it this way in the 1930s:

> The ruling passion of the age is to convert wealth into debt to derive a permanent future income from it – to convert wealth that perishes into debt that endures, debt that does not rot, costs nothing to maintain, and brings in perennial interest.
>
> (cited in Zence, 2009)

Money is surely mostly useful to everyone as a utility, a tool, it is meant to be a good servant to the economy, not its master. To put money first, to make it scarce (by storing it away) and charge for its use is an inversion of all that is good.

Just like any infrastructure created by past and present generations, money can be seen as a kind of commons, or at least a public utility. As such, perhaps its private enclosure ought to be subject to more conditions which create guidance for its issuance.

This would include devolving and diversifying money's powers and responsibilities whenever possible, so it can be locally or regionally discharged. It is a monoculture now as almost all our money (its creation and distribution) is centrally controlled.

An effective economic system embraces all scales – that is not only important for our productive infrastructure but also our money.

Interestingly, throughout history, all religions had an injunction against making money on money. All-important pre-Roman civilisations understood that debt was more and more onerous over time (debts grow by compound interest) and arranged periodic debt cancellation – what we still describe as a "debt jubilee".

There is then a huge precedent for debt jubilees but before we move to that, it is worth pausing to recognise here the work of anthropologist, David Graeber. His book '*Debt: The first 5000 years*' offers an illuminating insight into the history of debt and the impact its history continues to have on us today (Graeber, 2014).

If we look at today's economy, there is much merit to Graeber's assertions. Yesterday's debts are choking us. Debts are a claim on today's and tomorrow's wealth. We need a debt jubilee now for the simple reason – our debt overhang is so onerous that it is dampening spending in the productive economy.

"But how is it fair if *your* personal debts are cancelled and I don't have any," we hear you ask? There are moral and ethical entanglements throughout economics. Deciding what is fair is merely one of them. In this instance though, we see a 'fair to all' one off input of cash as an option. This reduces the indebtedness of those who owe money (it must be allocated to reducing debt) but gives those who don't have debts a cash injection – acting as an immediate boost to spending. Another might be a specific sector such as student debt or a revaluing of mortgages and payments adjustment.

As the physical world deals with a legacy of materials, energy, waste, and pollution, the monetary economy deals with the legacy of 'financial pollution' (Turner, 2017).

To ignore debt is like ignoring carbon already released into the atmosphere. You do so at your peril. The impacts are inevitable – they affect today and tomorrow. Like climate change, it requires reduced carbon emissions and a drawdown of what is there.

Rule 4: Build the commons & productive infrastructure at all scales

Many of the mental hangovers from the past century and beyond include thinking that what isn't private is state/city controlled – as if people cannot cooperatively manage resources. This has never been true. History is replete with examples of managing 'commons' (Walljasper, 2011). Being able to have, create and use resources in a distributed and collective sense makes it different ground than private or state.

'No commons without commoners' is the saying. A commons is not so much a thing as a process. These days, in practice, commons are often localised and used by smaller operations without much capital. These are frequently low cost or replicable – often both. But extensive land use arrangements in the past have been managed as commons and scale is not a barrier if governance issues can be worked through.

Today, the idea of the digital commons is getting attention. This matters. Building prosperity or wellbeing from the periphery is all about the possibilities that exist there – using what is available to add value. Investing in the right kind of enabling infrastructure that supports an enterprising approach

The future of cash at the heart of *The Wonderful Circles of Oz*

Our fictional narrative pivots around the role of cash (notes and coins) in an economy. This is about what cash means and the freedoms and obligations tied to it.

Cash need not derive from a nation but, like all money, must be acceptable. In return for its acceptance comes a benefit. It must be based on trust. It's an authority, social or legal, which protects its value and its 'currency' to flow through many exchanges.

Except in exceptional circumstances and with difficulty, money cannot be withdrawn. It is anonymous, it is a freedom to enter into an exchange for goods or services without interference or judgement.

Most importantly, it is not dependent on a digital infrastructure for its very existence. It still works if the lights go out.

And, for all cash's inconvenience, it is a principled and democratic technology. Human autonomy should not be at the whim of governance, which might decide to cut you off from the simplest of agencies – access to a medium of exchange or store of value.

Money is a visible manifestation of a community, of a managed commons and, for this book, a reminder that it is always more than economics.

is crucial – whether it is in the physical or digital realm. That enabling infrastructure may be places, spaces, tools, the land itself, or the sanctioning of more local or regional currencies or bonds. It is 'enabling' because the infrastructure allows a creative and enterprising response – it isn't being 'done' for people. The online *Commons Transition Primer* (P2P

Foundation, n.d.) is a great resource, sharing developed thinking and examples to make ideas of the Commons accessible.

In physical spaces, the commons infrastructure – around the likes of maker labs, community land trusts, municipal lots, and community kitchens – has a strong sense of being user managed.

There are many examples of digital commons too. Examples include platform cooperatives where the commons are its software. Often those involved get a stake in the data to which they have contributed.

Be they physical or digital though, as commons, they are neither privately nor state managed.

The role of government and governance

The activities of government, its governance, emerge then as a recurring theme. How a government uses money's power (via its creation and direction) cuts across all eight 'rules' we suggest to bring about change.

Governance basically sets the rules of the game. Appropriate governance then, is about providing the direction and enabling conditions for a thriving productive economy.

By addressing these four monetary rules (providing an adequate basic dividend, shifting taxes to penalise non-renewables, reducing personal debt, and guiding the issuance and destination of credit/money into productive and commons assets), government enables money to circulate effectively and can:

- Discourage lending into existing 'bubbly' assets, like real estate or shares, rather than production.
- Decrease inequality, which is based greatly on owning such 'bubbly' assets.
- Curb asset price inflation by redirecting the creation and rapid flow of money into natural and social capital.

- Increase employability and conserve mineral and manufactured 'stocks' through a shift in taxes.
- Boost disposable income and encourage spending in the productive economy.
- Encourage political stability by actively engaging citizens in the economy and democracy.

This flurry of ideas becomes meaningful when set in the economy's full context. There are two aspects – monetary and material. Circulation within both aspects is critical and, therefore, their 'circularity' implicit. To effectively circulate the whole, the system is more organic than mechanical, requiring us to recognise flows, stocks, and feedback.

Perhaps now we move to a place of recognition of what is already before us.

> We shall not cease from exploration, and the end of all our exploring will be to arrive where we started and know the place for the first time.
>
> (Eliot, 1943/2001)

References

Arthur, C. (2013, August 23). Tech Giants May Be Huge, But Nothing Matches Big Data. *The Guardian*. [online]. Available at https://www.theguardian.com/technology/2013/aug/23/tech-giants-data [Last accessed 11 May 2021].

Azmanova, A. (2020). *Capitalism on Edge: How Fighting Precarity Can Achieve Radical Change Without Crisis or Utopia*. New York: Columbia University Press.

Barnes, P. (2014). *With Liberty and Dividends for All: How to Save Our Middle Class When Jobs Don't Pay Enough*. San Francisco, CA: Berrett-Koehler Publishers.

Coady, D., Parry, I., Le, N. -P. and Shang, B. (2019). *Global Fossil Fuel Subsidies Remain Large: An Update Based on Country-Level Estimates*. IMF Working Paper WP/19/89, May 2019. Washington, DC: Fiscal Affairs Department, International Monetary Fund.

Cox, D. (2020). Canada's Forgotten Universal Basic Income Experiment. *BBC Worklife*. [online]. Available at https://www.bbc.com/worklife/article/20200624-canadas-forgotten-universal-basic-income-experiment [Last accessed 10 May 2021].
CRR. (2019). *The Crisis in Retailing – Check Latest Closures & Job Losses Centre for Retail Research*. [online]. Available at https://www.retailresearch.org/retail-crisis.html#:~:text=Our%20figures%20for%20store%20closures, losing%20sales%20to%20online%20shopping [Last accessed 10 May 2021].
Deutsche Telekom. (2017). *An Interview by Teledom.com with Guy Standing*. Communications Team of Deutsche Telekom, 13 November 2017. Bonn, Germany: Deutsche Telekom AG. [online]. Available at https://www.telekom.com/en/company/digital-responsibility/work/work/video-interview-with-guy-standing-506526 [Last accessed 10 May 2021].
Eliot, T. S. (1943/2001). Little Gidding. In *Four Quartets. Main edition*. London: Faber & Faber.
Graeber, D. (2014). *Debt: The First 5000 Years (Updated and Expanded Edition)*. New York: Melville House Publishing.
Groothuis, F, (2015, December 15). European Union (2016). *EX'Tax: Tax Pollution Not People*. [online]. Available at https://ex-tax.com/reports/new-era-new-plan-europe/ [Last accessed 11 May 2021].
Hudson, M. and Bezemer, D. (2016). Finance Is Not the Economy: Reviving the Conceptual Distinction. *Journal of Economic Issues, 50*(3), 745–768. https://doi.org/10.1080/00213624.2016.1210384.
Irfan, U. (2019, May 17). Fossil Fuels Are Underpriced by a Whopping $5.2 Trillion. *Vox*. [online]. Available at https://www.vox.com/2019/5/17/18624740/fossil-fuel-subsidies-climate-imf [Last accessed 11 May 2021].
Kay, J. (2012, November 21). The Monumental Folly of Rent-Seeking. [Online]. Available at https://www.johnkay.com/2012/11/21/the-monumental-folly-of-rent-seeking/ [Last accessed 10 May 2021].
Kelton, S. (2020). *The Deficit Myth: Modern Monetary Theory and How to Build a Better Economy*. London: John Murray (Publishers).
Liberto, D. (2021, January 27). The Wealth Effect Investopedia. [online]. Available at https://www.investopedia.com/terms/w/wealtheffect.asp [Last accessed 10 May 2021].
LVT Fan's Blog. (2020, March 31). The Single Tax: An Essay on the Single Tax in 50 Words. [online blog]. Available at https://lvtfan.

typepad.com/lvtfans_blog/natural-monopolies/ [Last accessed 11 May 2021].

Mazzucato, M. (2021). *Mission Economy: A Moonshot Guide to Changing Capitalism*. Dublin: Allen Lane/Penguin Random House.

Nazir, S. (2019, December 30). Over 140,000 Jobs Have Been Lost This Year. *Retail Gazette*. [online]. Available at https://www.retail-gazette.co.uk/blog/2019/12/140000-jobs-lost-year/ [Last accessed 10 May 2021].

P2P Foundation. (n.d.). *The Commons Transition Primer: Welcome*. [online]. Available at www.primer.commonstransition.org [Last accessed 11 May 2021].

Pettifor, A. (2019). *The Case for the Green New Deal*. New York: Verso.

Pimentel, D. A. V., Aymar, I. M. and Lawson, M. (2018). *Reward Work, Not Wealth: To End the Inequality Crisis, We Must Build an Economy for Ordinary Working People, Not the Rich and Powerful*. [English Version]. Oxford: Oxfam International. Available at https://oi-files-d8-prod.s3.eu-west-2.amazonaws.com/s3fs-public/file_attachments/bp-reward-work-not-wealth-220118-en.pdf [Last accessed 10 May 2021].

PYMNTS (2019, February 21). *UK Government Report Calls on eCommerce Players to Pay More Taxes*. [online]. Available at https://www.pymnts.com/news/ecommerce/2019/uk-report-ecommerce-taxes/ [Last accessed 11 May 2021].

Roberts, M. (2010, January 29). Overproduction and Capitalist Crisis. [online]. Available at https://thenextrecession.wordpress.com/2010/01/29/overproduction-and-capitalist-crisis/ [Last accessed 10 May 2021].

Stahel, W. R. (2011). The Virtuous Circle? Sustainable Economics and Taxation in a Time of Austerity. *Thinkpiece CII*, 63. October. The Chartered Insurance Institute. [online]. Available at http://www.businessperformance.org/sites/default/files/tp63_stahel_sustainable_taxation_10oct2011_4.pdf [Last accessed 26 June 2021].

The Money Charity. (2019). Money Statistics December 2019. [online]. Available at https://themoneycharity.org.uk/money-statistics/december-2019/ [Last accessed 11 May 2021]

Turner, A. (2017). *Between Debt and the Devil: Money, Credit, and Fixing Global Finance*. Princeton, NJ: Princeton University Press.

Walljasper, J. (2011, October 02). Elinor Ostrom's 8 Principles for Managing Commons. *On the Commons*. [online]. Available at https://

www.onthecommons.org/magazine/elinor-ostroms-8-principles-managing-commmons [Last accessed 11 May 2021].
Yang, A. (2020). *The Freedom Dividend*. Yang2020.com [online] https://2020.yang2020.com/policies/the-freedom-dividend/.
Zencey, E. (2009, April 11). Mr. Soddy's Ecological Economy. *The New York Times*. [online]. Available at https://www.nytimes.com/2009/04/12/opinion/12zencey.html?_r=1&ref=opinion [Last accessed 11 May 2021].

23 The liberation and terrors of a digital world

> We worship innovation for its ability to advance us. Yet innovation that extracts, exploits and excludes does not solve societal problems or advance collective wealth. In fact, it does the opposite.
>
> Ken & Alex

Knowledge, our economy's life force, animates everything it touches and provides our richest source of feedback… information. After many economic cycles, this knowledge, should we choose to listen, informs us – then we can adjust the 'rules of the game'. There is potential to change our economy's form – for it to become circular, circulating, and regenerative.

Like alchemy, these adjustments are iterative, with learnings revealed by the experience of the economic process itself. Digital has already proven itself to be a change accelerator and one that is only just getting started. Tech's transforming how our economy ticks. Tech will see the economy and those it serves flourish or fail but all that is dependent on (hu)man, not machine.

Microsoft CLO, Brad Smith, co-authored the book 'Tools and Weapons' (Smith and Browne, 2019) and the title is a good metaphor. Change driven by tech is inevitable but how we choose to use it is not. Ultimately, how we respond will determine whether tech's economic impact widens or narrows systemic inequality.

The world has always faced change though, so why is technology seemingly having such a big economic impact and doing so

DOI: 10.4324/9781003217657-26

with such pace? Tech is revolutionising by doing three mutually reinforcing things simultaneously:

1. Becoming general purpose – As different technologies converge, tech's global reach is both broad and deep.
2. Making market access easier – Precision automation coupled with AI is crashing the price of production and distribution.
3. Directly connecting people, places, and things – goodbye middleman. Platforms enable direct connection to audiences.

The liberation and terrors of becoming general purpose

The digital revolution is the coming together of numerous technologies to become one, general purpose, technology explains Jeremy Rifkin. Rifkin's an American economic and social theorist who has written extensively about the impact of scientific and technological changes (e.g., Rifkin, 2014).

The smartphone, for example, integrates six technologies (most of them, incidentally, developed in the public realm). Although originally seen as a business tool because of its high cost and complex application, public demand quickly outpaced corporate demand because of its usefulness (Sarwar and Soomro, 2013). Today, nearly 84% of the world's population own a smartphone, and six years ago, it was just under 50% (Turner, 2021).

What futurist Azeem Azhar (2021) calls Exponential Technology (in recognition of the accelerating speed of change as well as its combining of different elements), is now everywhere. It is changing the game within traditional 'non tech' industries and its general application is impacting culture and social life. Just think what *Airbnb* has done to the hotel industry – despite not owning a single room, or what *Uber*'s done to the taxi sector – without owning any vehicles, or what

Netflix has done to the media industry – long before it started producing its own content.

The digital sector is still just 7.7% of the UK's economy but its growth is outstripping the economy as a whole six-fold and is set to continue its upward trajectory (Warman, 2020).

It's a similar story elsewhere in the world, with Microsoft's Chairman and CEO, Satya Nadella, citing in their 2020 annual report "technology spending as a percentage of gross domestic product is projected to double" (Nadella, 2020).

His letter within that report is insightful, so we summarise and share some of its salient points here:

> Confronted by the year's compounding crises – including coronavirus and the economic crisis – we became digital first responders to the world's first responders. Supporting those from healthcare, to education, to public sector, to critical manufacturing, grocery, and retail. Tech has helped organizations not only stay open for business but innovate. We've witnessed years of digital transformation in mere months and the world's now at an inflection point, with digital tech set to define what comes next.

So, while today's tech may be less than 10% of GDP, what's set to expedite its growth is how other sectors, in every aspect of our lives, come to apply and rely on it.

"Digital technology is the most malleable tool ever created," says Nadella and, of course, "Microsoft's key to building the technologies that will empower every person and every organization on the planet" (Nadella, 2020).

The upside to tech becoming general purpose is digital giants use those economies of scale to deliver excellent digital tools for the global world. Imagine a coronavirus-style lockdown without the benefits of technology.

But making a return on such huge technological investments is difficult without the controlling market share. Inevitably, 'being number one' is replaced with 'being the only one'.

The liberation and terrors of making market access easier

Precision automation coupled with AI is crashing the price of production and distribution. For established agile players, who embrace tech and the change it forces, there is plenty to play for. Professional services consultancy PwC (Pricewaterhouse-Coopers) suggest AI alone will lift global GDP by 14% in the next decade (Rao and Verweij, 2017, p. 4). But mature players, often busy defending existing markets, find it hard to embrace disruptive innovation. Half the Fortune 500 companies from 2006 no longer exist (DDI, 2018, p. 12).

Machines have extended the reach of our bodies for centuries. Automated factories transformed the world of work by producing more stuff with less staff. But today's digital revolution extends machine muscle into mental power. And it is tech's cognitive mastery that is a workplace game changer according to renowned author Yuval Harari (2019).

The shadow side of machines having muscle and mental capacity is that tech is disrupting worldwide workforces regardless of sector – particularly the skills people need for employment, the jobs they do, and how they are employed to do them.

Enabled by technology, the swing towards contractors, freelancers, giggers, and crowd workers has been seismic. Freelancers, for example, are the fastest-growing labour group in the EU (Volini et al., 2019).

For those with highly sought skills, 'alternative working' enables flexible, portfolio careers filled with varied and interesting work. But that is not a representative picture and the economy's already sending clear signals.

Forty years ago, wages started losing touch with economic growth. Since then, profitability has increased but wages have stagnated. Economic growth has largely been backfilled by, part time, poorly paid, precarious, employment with little protections for the 'alternative' workers on which it draws. And "these workers do not make confident consumers" (Webster, 2017).

With good reason. As the coronavirus crisis has most recently shown, these alternative workers were quickly abandoned and they fell into penury.

People's purchasing power in a book about the future success of our productive economy is a critical question.

'Automation has already shown it disproportionately reduces demand for less skilled workers, with innovation favouring the more educated' (World Bank Group, 2019, p. 29). But as tech revolutionises, signals already suggest those wanted for future work will have skills in increasingly concentrated areas.

There might well be, as the World Economic Forum suggests, a "reskilling imperative" (Leopold et al., 2018), but who pays, and will today's and tomorrow's workforce be willing or able to 'reskill' into such concentrated employment areas in an ageing world?

Tech can speed supply in the productive economy but, on its current transformational trajectory of the labour market and earned income, it might just destroy demand.

So, we need to think carefully about people's purchasing power in our future economy (a basic dividend, a tax shift and a debt jubilee all speak to this) but we also need to think beyond that... to people's purpose, psychology, protections, and prosperity in an economy transformed by tech. And, while it is not for this book, we must also recognise the repercussions (economic and otherwise) this technology has on people beyond the world of work. Those implications reach back to childhood, starting with what and how we teach our young people in this 'half-life of skills' era.

The liberation and terrors of directly connecting people, places, and things

Goodbye middleman. Digital platforms are replacing our reliance on traditional intermediaries. We can now directly connect with people, places, and things regardless of their physical location.

Via platform technology, anyone with a smartphone can reach people anywhere and create demand for their products or services. With a smartphone and a connection, anyone has a tool for business or social good with immediate and immense flexibility. And, we don't need to look far to see the transformative power these connecting platforms offer. In 2017, British YouTuber Daniel Middleton (DanTDM) reportedly became the channel's highest earner – making over £12m from the video sharing site (Andrews, 2020).

At the other end of the spectrum, that same platform technology is being used for social good by sharing open-source data to benefit local communities. Take *FareShare Go* in the UK for example (FareShare, 2020). This tech platform takes data from supermarkets and the UK charity food redistribution market. *FareShare* matches a charity with a local supermarket with surplus edible food. The charity collects food that would otherwise be binned and instead puts it to good use. Since 2015, 7,500 charities have benefited (Calnana, 2018) connecting with more than 3,500 supermarket stores.

Digital has created a new 'information commons' and people have been quick to recognise its transformational power – likening it to the discovery of oil reserves in the previous era.

It should hardly be surprising then that, just as we've seen the enclosing of the commons in the physical world, there's a similar scramble going on in the virtual world. We're literally seeing history repeat itself.

Today's reality is that a handful of firms dominate the digital sector. Just think about businesses built on platform technology. *Facebook*, which connects you to your friends, reported 1.93 billion daily active users in the third quarter of 2021. *Google*, connecting you to the world's information, had 92% market share as of January 2021. *Amazon*, connecting you to products and services, became the second $1 trillion business in 2018, after *Apple* and, during the last quarter of 2020 recorded sales of more than $100 billion for the first time. And, of course, both *Apple* and *Microsoft* are the tech titans connecting your hardware to software to access all world wide web applications.

The digital economy is mirroring the enclosure and consolidation we've seen in the 'real-world' economy. It means swapping 'making' with 'taking' or replacing production with rent seeking... again.

A digital model that replicates efficiency and scale with the hope that something good will fall out is flawed. It is based on the same simplified, standardised, volume-throughput model we have created in our physical world, which has proven itself an unequal and brittle system.

Yet, technology gives us the opportunity to improve circulation within the virtual- and real- world economy by enabling a new layer of connections focused not on profit but exchange – just think about that *FareShare Go* example.

That new connecting layer can only happen though if the platform or other tech enabling it does not become completely gated by a dominant few.

Platform cooperatives, designed to meet an economic, social, or cultural need, return benefits to users and enable new connections within the economy encouraging circulation.

With the acceleration of materials platforms like *www.materiom.org*, 3D printing, maker and hacker labs, and community kitchens, some write about the rise of the real sharing economy, shareable cities, or how non-profits will rule the world. And certainly, with the decline in formal employment such digital enablement that leads to a wealth of 'socially produced goods and services' (Mason, 2019) at all scales would be most welcome – especially when accompanied by the important monetary tools already discussed like a basic dividend and a tax shift.

But, while the cost of a smartphone and connection have dropped to make such a vision technically possible, the huge capital investments needed to build the enabling applications remain out of reach to most. Without commons-biased digital infrastructure investments, user interfaces are less advanced. That means people tend to migrate towards offers by the usual dominating industry suspects for reasons of efficiency and convenience – perpetuating the cycle towards digital's further enclosure by the dominant few.

In exchange for access to gigantic platformed communities of connection and information, we freely give up masses of personal data with little transparency from tech companies on how they use it. And, perhaps, we don't mind so much if those companies mine our data to get us to buy *Aquafresh* over *Colgate*, or even a *VW* over a *Ford*. But what if that data is weaponised and eats away at the very heart of our democracy?

In our earlier narrative 'the nightmare of Oz the Terrible', we fictionalise Sesame Credit and how this might overtly play out further. There's more detail about our fictionalisation of Sesame Credit and its application in the real world in Part 3 'Sesame and Social credit systems'. But, if you want to be truly terrified about the art of covert manipulation, just look at the work of Observer investigative journalist, Carole Cadwalladr (e.g., her TED Talk, 2019) or Christopher Wylie's extraordinary book 'Mindf*ck'.

Who guards the guards or, in this case, the gatekeepers of vast gatekept digital communities? As Wylie and Cadwalladr discovered, 'in the digital realm where complex technological crimes happen at global scale beyond any single jurisdiction', the answer still seems to be no one (Wylie, 2020). We come onto look further at democracy in this book's final chapter, but for now, let's return to digital's potential to liberate a circular economy.

A circular economy enables the recreation of elegant abundance evident in living systems. That is economic growth but not as we define it today. It has much more to do with quality of life than merely throughput. It's about the shape of the economy, not its size, as Ann Pettifor (2019) has noted.

To illustrate this point, let's again momentarily return to the fictional part of this book – to where we found our Nexus 209 in the clearing of a wood. Rather than focus on the AI though, let's switch our attention to the wood because trees and their surroundings offer a perfect example of how a networked, complex, exchange-based living system effectively operates.

The tree trunk and branches provide structure and flow for materials and money in our economy. But the twigs, leaves, filial roots, and tendrils are 'exchange' focused on creating and sourcing the nutrients the tree needs.

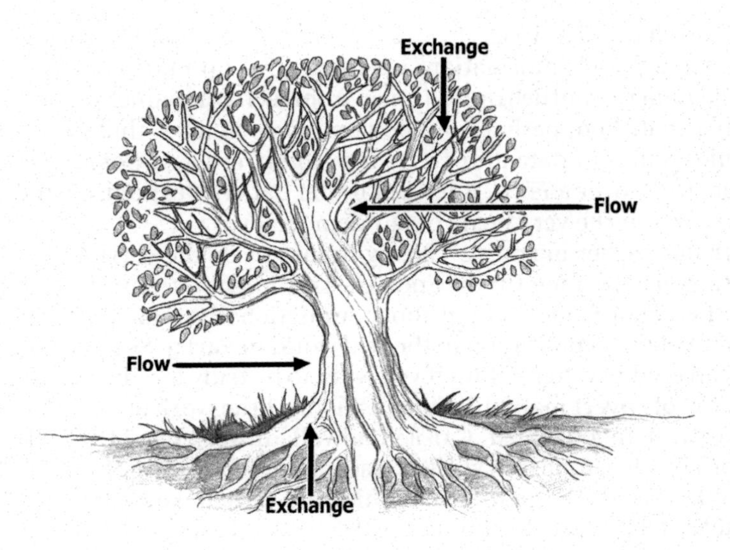

The first thing we learn is that there is an abundance of exchanges – there are a lot of leaves, for example, on a tree. A myriad of roots too. That tells us a tree has redundancy built in.

To aid a tree's resilience though, and that of the wider forest ecosystem upon which its survival depends, it also exchanges information with neighbouring trees. It does this through an underground layer of fungal exchange networks. It is something German forester and author, Peter Wohlleben, says others are aptly calling 'the wood-wide-web'.

> Trees share water and nutrients through these exchange networks and use them to communicate. They send distress signals to each other about drought, disease, and insect attacks. When exchanging these messages, nearby trees alter their behaviour, helping provide resilience to shocks.
>
> (Wohlleben, 2016)

In an exact parallel to the internet, a forest is a myriad of complex, expanding, frequently self-learning networks facilitating an abundance of exchanges – feeding and protecting individual trees and the wider collective wood in which they grow.

For a forest to thrive, it needs more than a tiny clump of standalone, single species, giant, trees. These tree trunks and their branches provide stability and structure, but a healthy forest also needs diversity and exchange in abundance to fully flow and circulate. Just as invisible fungal networks provide the fertile floor upon which all forest life is built, we need digital to be a golden thread, that weaves an abundance of exchanges through our economy and into the fabric of our times.

What living systems show us is that effective systems combine economies of scope, formed by variety, with economies of scale, which are the bigger structures and flows. The coronavirus has shown that we have the balance wrong – resilience is low, too much rests on long supply chains, which proves brittle.

This is tragic because digital makes production and exchange potentially more efficient for local producers and for those selling limited quantities than ever before. A variety of smaller volume products from one region, network or business, result in multiple cashflows – offering smaller producers' greater resilience.

In a digitally enabled devolved and distributed world, volume and scale become less important than connection to local markets. Platform technology allows the efficient sale or exchange of waste and by-product. After all, one person's waste is another person's treasure. It means, with limited investment and minimal energy, smaller producers can flip costly 'waste' into additional revenue streams by selling it as 'food' into another's production cycle.

For Gunter Pauli, the circular economy business entrepreneur and author of *The Blue Economy*, adding value rather than focusing on lowering costs is fundamental (Gunter, 2017). Adding and circulating value with what is already available provides multiple benefits in a 'fair to all' competitive environment. This means fewer economic rents can be earned, and multiple cashflows provide multiple possibilities for yet more entrepreneurial initiative.

Pauli advocates that these multiple benefits are the unlock to a local 'double digit growth model' that responds to basic needs, with local products and services that circulate cash in the local economy.

It seems there are two opposing approaches, but what living systems teach us is that it isn't local versus global, scope versus scale, or variety versus volume – it is their co-existence that creates an abundance of value. Big firms need customers, and to be customers those people need an income. In a working world disrupted by digital with a shift to 'alternative' working, these people also need tools, connectivity, and access to the commons.

Digital technologies are central to that process, which by design and intention, and with time and many failures, can evolve to produce a system wide effectiveness. Neither efficiency nor resilience on their own gives an optimal result. Only the appropriate relationship between the two provides effectiveness.

As in all systems built by iteration, by feedback, the rules of the relationships are the key. Over time, they generate desirable patterns or can be adjusted to do so. Complexity is usually an outcome of the iteration of simple rules.

Returning then to the earlier illustration by Sally Goerner et al. (Fullerton, 2015) as to what makes an effective system, we see the shape of the curve is a clue. The curve weighs towards resilience. The bias is towards the network rather than the hierarchy. These patterns around scale are remarkably consistent.

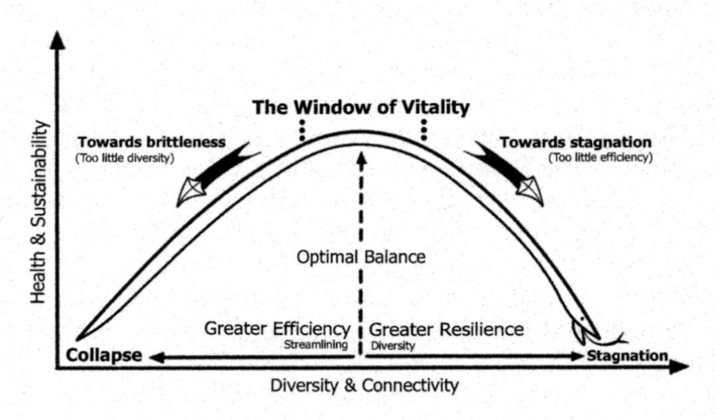

The window of vitality. Adapted from Sally Goerner, Bernard Lietaer, Bob Ulanowicz (Ulanowicz et al. 2009).

From organisms to corporations to cities, scientist and writer, Geoffrey West (2018) has been impressed by the regularity in which these systems scale. The pattern which biases towards the network rather than the hierarchy seems to be a marker, a general characteristic, of all such systems. So why not the economy? Or perhaps the better question is, why wouldn't we view our economic system in this way too?

In the body, there are many more capillaries than veins and arteries. In a forest, there are more leaves, twigs, filial roots than tree trunks and branches. If cities and corporations have similar scale relationships, then perhaps this is a clue to how we can support the economy. Maybe our economy simply cannot work optimally otherwise.

What is less clear is who our economy is designed to serve. And, it is with this front of mind that in the next chapter, we explore democracy and the conundrum of power and control in these kinds of complex and dynamic economic systems.

References

Andrews, J. (2020, May 28). How to make money from YouTube – and how much you get paid per view (Updated Version). *Daily Mirror.* [online]. Available at https://www.mirror.co.uk/money/how-make-money-youtube-how-12650536 [Last accessed 11 May 2021].

Azhar, A. (2021). *Exponential – How Accelerating Technology Is Leaving Us Behind and What to Do About It.* London: Random House Business.

Cadwalladr, C. (2019, June 10). Facebook's Role in Brexit – and the Threat to Democracy. *TED Talk.* [online]. Available at https://www.ted.com/talks/carole_cadwalladr_facebook_s_role_in_brexit_and_the_threat_to_democracy.

Calnana, M. (2018, April 24). Waitrose to Extend Use of Fare Share Go App [online]. Available at https://www.thegrocer.co.uk/food-waste/waitrose-to-extend-use-of-fareshare-go-app-across-its-estate/566258.article [Last accessed 11 May 2021].

DDI. (2018). Global Leadership Forecast 2018. In *RESEARCH: 25 Research Findings about the State, Context, and Future of Leadership.* Bridgeville, PA: Development Dimensions International. [online].

Available at https://www.ddiworld.com/research/global-leadership-forecast-2018 [Last accessed 11 May 2021].

FareShare. (2020). About FareShare [online]. Available at https://fareshare.org.uk/wp-content/uploads/2020/02/User-Co-ordinator.pdf and this is good too [Last accessed 11 May 2021].

Fullerton, J. (2015). *Regenerative Capitalism. How Universal Principles and Patterns Will Shape Our New Economy.* [online]. Available at http://capitalinstitute.org/wp-content/uploads/2015/04/2015-Regenerative-Capitalism-4-20-15-final.pdf [Last accessed 10 May 2021].

Gunter, P. (2017). *The Blue Economy 3.0: The Marriage of Science, Innovation and Entrepreneurship Creates a New Business Model that Transforms Society.* Bloomington, IN: XLIBRIS.

Harari, Y. N. (2019). *21 Lessons for the 21st Century.* London: Vintage.

Leopold, T. A., Ratcheva, V. and Zahidi, S. (2018). *The Future of Jobs Report* 2018. Insight Report, Centre for the New Economy and Society, World Economic Forum. September 2018. [online]. Available at http://www3.weforum.org/docs/WEF_Future_of_Jobs_2018.pdf [Last accessed 11 May 2021].

Mason. P. (2019, July 01). Time for Postcapitalism. *Social Europe.* [online]. Available at https://www.socialeurope.eu/time-for-post-capitalism [Last accessed 11 May 2021].

Nadella, S. (2020). Our Opportunity to Define the World We Want to Live In. [online]. Available at https://www.linkedin.com/pulse/our-opportunity-define-world-we-want-live-satya-nadella/ [Last accessed 03 September 2021].

Pettifor, A. (2019). *The Case for the Green New Deal.* New York: Verso.

Rao, A. S. and Verweij, G. (2017). Sizing the Prize: what's the Real Value of AI for Your Business and How Can You Capitalise? *London PricewaterhouseCoopers.* [online]. Available at https://www.pwc.com/gx/en/issues/analytics/assets/pwc-ai-analysis-sizing-the-prize-report.pdf [Last accessed 11 May 2021].

Rifkin, J. (2014). *The Zero Marginal Cost Society: The Internet of Things, the Collaborative Commons, and the Eclipse of Capitalism.* New York: Palgrave Macmillan.

Sarwar, M. and Soomro, T. R. (2013). Impact of Smartphone's on Society. *European Journal of Scientific Research, 89*(2), 216–226. Available at https://www.researchgate.net/publication/236669025_Impact_of_Smartphone%27s_on_Society [Last accessed 11 May 2021].

Smith, B. and Browne C. A. (2019). *Tools and Weapons: The Promise and Peril of the Digital Age*. London: Hodder & Stoughton.

Turner, A. (2021, June). How Many Smartphones Are in the World? June 2021 Mobile User Statistics: Discover the Number of Phones in the World & Smartphone Penetration by Country or Region. *bankmycell*. [online]. Available at https://www.bankmycell.com/blog/how-many-phones-are-in-the-world [Last accessed 07 January 2022].

Ulanowicz, E. R. Goerner, S. Lietaer, B. and Gomez, R. (2009). Quantifying Sustainability: Resilience, Efficiency and the Return of Information Theory. *Ecological Complexity, 6*(1), 27–36. doi:10.1016/j.ecocom.2008.10.005.

Volini, E., Schwartz, J., Roy, I., Hauptmann, M., van Durme, Y., Denny, B. and Berson, J. (2019). *Leading the Social Enterprise: Reinvent with a Human Focus 2019*. Deloitte Global Human Capital Trends Report. [online]. Available at https://www2.deloitte.com/content/dam/insights/us/articles/5136_HC-Trends-2019/DI_HC-Trends-2019.pdf [Last accessed 11 May 2021].

Warman, M. (2020, February). Digital Sector Worth More Than £400 Million a Day to UK Economy. *From the Department for Digital, Culture, Media & Sport*. [online]. Available at https://www.gov.uk/government/news/digital-sector-worth-more-than-400-million-a-day-to-uk-economy [Last accessed 03 September 2021].

Webster, K. (2017). *The Circular Economy: A Wealth of Flows, second edition*. Cowes, Isle of Wight: Ellen MacArthur Foundation.

West, G. (2018). *Scale: The Universal Laws of Life and Death in Organisms, Cities and Companies*. London: Weidenfeld and Nicholson.

Wohlleben, P. (2016). *The Hidden Life of Trees: What They Feel, How They Communicate*. Vancouver, BC, Canada: Greystone Books. Cited R. Grant (2018). Do Trees Talk to Each Other? A Controversial German Forester Says Yes, and His Ideas Are Shaking Up the Scientific World. *Ask Smithsonian, Smithsonian Magazine*, March 2018. [online]. Available at https://www.smithsonianmag.com/science-nature/the-whispering-trees-180968084/ [Last accessed 11 May 2021]. Copyright 2018 Smithsonian Institution. Reprinted with permission from Smithsonian Enterprises. All rights reserved. Reproduction in any medium is strictly prohibited without permission from Smithsonian magazine.

World Bank Group. (2019). *World Development Report 2019: The Changing Nature of Work*. Washington, DC: The International

Bank for Construction and Redevelopment/World Bank (English Version). Available at https://openknowledge.worldbank.org/handle/10986/30435 [Last accessed 27 June 2021].
Wylie, C. (2020). *Mindf*ck: Inside Cambridge Analytica's Plot to Break the World*. London: Profile Books.

24 A flourishing democracy – the path to a flourishing economy

We have to recognize that human flourishing is not a mechanical process; it's an organic process... All you can do, like a farmer, is create the conditions under which they will begin to flourish.

Sir Ken Robinson, *Bringing on the Learning Revolution*, TED Talk (2010)

Paradigm ➡ structure ➡ pattern ➡ events

Donella Meadows was a pioneer of systems thinking. In essence, we aspire to be systems thinkers as it's a way of thinking that gives us the freedom to identify the root causes of problems and see new opportunities. Like Meadows in her core text *Thinking in Systems*, we feel there is a sequence from **paradigm** or shared vision (the almost unconscious set of assumptions we use in our everyday thinking – usually metaphor based), through **structures** and how we frame our thinking. This allows us to see **patterns** of related events and finally to examine **events.** Synthesis precedes analysis.

In looking around at the many issues confronting us, we've strived to uncover the systemic approaches to change with the two cycles around assets and finance (the gatekept cycle) and the materials and energy cycle (the productive cycle). Yet, governance is just as important. An economy might do very well

DOI: 10.4324/9781003217657-27

in terms of output and working within planetary boundaries – you could say it is 'flourishing' – but it could be a slave state, a feudal fiefdom, a totalitarian regime, a 'free for all' market dystopia. Or, it could be a system in service to all. Democracy is the given term but democracy as it exists is very fragile – often a first-past-the-post representative democracy with all its familiar issues.

Just as the control of access to commons resources in relatively few hands clots our economic system, control of political access and decision making in relatively few hands clogs democracy.

There is an intrinsic link between a flourishing democracy and a flourishing economy. For the question isn't only 'how' we evolve our economic system but 'who decides' and this requires, in our view, a reinvigorated democracy. Both our economy and democracy are interdependent 'living' (non-linear, feedback rich) systems that need to be multiscale, brimming with diverse and active agents that create and circulate value (and Values) from the very periphery of society right through to the core.

But democracy today is far from 'active'. The late, British Prime Minister, Margaret Thatcher, (in)famously said: 'There is no such thing as society' (Thatcher, 1987). This 'catchy' phrase took hold, and not only within the UK. Framed by a story, with democratic roots, people began to see themselves only as individuals. Vast swathes of common inheritance were enclosed based on a social contract which with privatisation meant efficiency through competition and, for the individual, the harder you work, the higher your reward. Over time, many disengaged from society, their local communities and politics altogether.

As Kim Stanley Robinson (2020) articulately notes in his article in The New Yorker:

> We are individuals first, yes, just as bees are, but we exist in a larger social body. Society is not only real; it's fundamental. We can't live without it... Even as an individual, you are a biome, an ecosystem much like a forest or a swamp

> or a coral reef. Your skin holds inside all kinds of unlikely cooperations, and to survive you depend on any number of interspecies operations going on within you all at once. We are societies made of societies, there are nothing but societies.

There's competition in nature but not at the expense of all else – relationships are symbiotic. In the swing to individualism, set against a backdrop where there's no such thing as "society", our "societal" contract has broken – its original mutuality abandoned. The resulting devastation broadens this from an economic debate to an ethical one, about the type of society we collectively want to live in – something that strikes at the very heart of democracy.

Today's democratic decision making looks as crude as an economy designed as pipework. It was conceived in an era of four-yearly ballot boxes, limited economic and political literacy, national (or in the EU's case pan-national) decision making, with active consumerism encouraged and enabled over active citizenship.

Democracy has become enfeebled by the notion that an occasional decision to select a political party or figurehead is all the participation citizens need. Yet, those parties or figureheads often lack diversity and share the same economic understandings, the same theory, and the same tired juxtaposing of labour and capital.

According to environmental and political activist and writer, George Monbiot, "Democracy becomes fainter as scale increases. The larger the scale of any form of politics, the harder it is to ensure that popular control remains a live proposition." (Monbiot, 2017, P130).

Politics then, like all living systems, including our economy, requires exchange at all scales to remain healthy. For it is exchange at all scales that enables circulation and creates abundance. And, according to economist Herman Daly (2019), 'abundance and excess capacity is a prerequisite for freedom and democracy'.

Democracy needs an active political periphery where powers and responsibilities are devolved – "handed to the smallest political unit that can reasonably discharge them" (Monbiot, 2017, P130). That reinvigorates democracy, people become citizens and producers as well as consumers. Many more participate in their own lives and communities, rather than reside as passive consumers dependent on work. Networked in 'schools of democracy' – a phrase used by Michel Bauwens in the peer-to-peer sharing economy – enabled predominately via a digitally platformed commons (see Sylvester-Bradley, 2017).

It is our active involvement in the commons that can ignite grassroots development where people regain power to make decisions, priorities, and choices in a participatory manner.

In nature, it is the scale, quality, and mutualistic nature of relationships that matter – perhaps this too offers insight for achieving more active relationships and participation between government, economic policy, and wider society. It's about two-way dialogue and an abundance of new 'nodes'. New nodes, for example, like the emergence of "citizen assemblies" or what the RSA's CEO Matthew Taylor refers to as 'citizen deliberative democracy' (Taylor, 2019). And perhaps too, borrowing the concept from other disciplines, "citizen economists" – those with economics knowledge between expert and amateur who act as lynchpins by relating knowledge and practice in an informed way. But whatever their form, these communications and relationships become plentiful and symbiotic at different scales – just like that in the forest.

Guy Standing (2017) has made the case for celebrating and reminding people of England's *Charter of the Forest* in 1217. Just as Magna Carta began the slow progress around human rights, the Forest Charter should serve to remind us about the commons. Our 'forests' are a source of wealth and wellbeing to which we all have rights of access – freedom and autonomy are distributive by design.

And most recently, as Kate Raworth (2020) reminds us, our new economy will be 'regenerative and distributive by design'. What it won't be based on is reluctant redistribution handouts because there are no commons left to access. For it is the commons and our participation in them that helps us meet what Maslow (1943, 1954) describes as our basic needs – they help avoid our becoming slaves to wages or welfare.

To avoid furthering unequal opportunity, widening income inequality, and rising societal unrest, we must build our social contract of the future on a productive, circular economy, where wealth is created at all scales, underpinned by an active democracy that more equitably circulates and distributes. We have new freedoms and autonomy because of:

- An adequate basic dividend which is a fair return on our enclosed commonwealth resources, together with access to more historical and newly created commons. A right, not a handout.
- A shift in taxes towards non-renewables and away from people and productive profits.
- Relieving people of their debt burden with a debt jubilee or for those without debt, giving a spending boost.
- Business opportunities from the investment in productive infrastructure at all scales based on turning waste into food and adding value with what we have.

The story of the new economy is all about rebuilding capitals through circulation. It is based within a systems framework and appreciates the commons; the data and its tools; the abundance of the earth's endowment; the distributed renewable energy sources; the re-invention of money; and access to the historical and ongoing commons. Then, what we call civilization can start to re-emerge in a new form. It is based on environmental and economic as well as social justice.

As economist Eric Beinhocker says:

> ...economics has painted itself as a detached amoral science, but humans are moral creatures. We must bring morality back into the centre of economics for people to relate and trust it. All the science shows that deeply

> ingrained, reciprocal moral behaviours are the glue that holds society together. Understanding the economy as not just an amoral machine that provides incentives and distributes resources, but rather as a human moral construct is essential, not just for creating a more just economy, but also for understanding how the economy actually creates prosperity....
>
> (Beinhocker, 2017)

...and, these authors would add: for understanding how to revitalise democracy.

References

Beinhocker, E. (2017, January 31). It's Time for a New Economic Thinking Based on the Best Science Available, Not Ideology. A New Narrative for a Complex Age. *Evonomics: The Next Evolution of Economics*. [online]. Available at https://evonomics.com/time-new-economic-thinking-based-best-science-available-not-ideology/ [Last accessed 11 May 2021].

Daly, H. (2019). Envisioning a Successful Steady-State Economy. *Journal of Population & Sustainability, 3*(1), (Autumn/Winter 2018), 21–33. Available at https://jpopsus.org/wp-content/uploads/2019/02/Daly-JPS-Vol3-No1-2018.pdf [Last accessed 11 May 2021].

Maslow, A. H. (1943). A Theory of Human Motivation. *Psychological Review, 50*(4), 370–396. https://doi.org/10.1037/h0054346.

Maslow, A. H. (1954). The Instinctoid Nature of Basic Needs. *Journal of Personality, 22*(3), 326–347. https://doi.org/10.1111/j.1467-6494.1954.tb01136.x.

Monbiot, G. (2017). *Out of the Wreckage: A New Politics for an Age of Crisis*. London: Verso.

Raworth, K. (2020). Speaking at the On-Life Seminar: Designing a Regenerative and Distributive Economy. *The Economy of Francesco*, 21 May 2020. [YouTube]. Available at https://www.youtube.com/watch?v=vHcx-9JTvIE [Last accessed 11 May 2021].

Robinson, K. (2010). Bring on the Learning Revolution! TED talk. To Watch the Full Talk Visit https://www.ted.com/talks/sir_ken_robinson_bring_on_the_learning_revolution. Cited in O. Friedman (2020, August 22). Remembering Sir Ken Robinson.

TED Blog. [online]. Available at https://blog.ted.com/remembering-sir-ken-robinson/ [Last accessed 07 January 2022].

Robinson, K. S. (2020, May 01). The Coronavirus Is Rewriting Our Imaginations. What Felt Impossible Has Become Thinkable. The Spring of 2020 Is Suggestive of How Much, and How Quickly, We Can Change as a Civilization. *The New Yorker: Annals of Inquiry*. [online]. Available at https://www.newyorker.com/culture/annals-of-inquiry/the-coronavirus-and-our-future © Conde Nast. [Last accessed 03 September 2021].

Standing, G. (2017, November 06). *Why You've Never Heard of a Charter That's as Important as the Magna Carta*. Open Democracy UK. [online]. Available at https://www.opendemocracy.net/en/opendemocracyuk/why-youve-never-heard-of-charter-thats-as-important-as-magna-carta/ [Last accessed 11 May 2021].

Sylvester-Bradley, O. (2017, January 13). Representation Is No Longer Enough – a Q&A with Michel Bauwens. *Open Democracy*. [online]. Available at https://www.opendemocracy.net/en/representation-is-no-longer-enough-qa-with-michel-bauwens/ [Last accessed 11 May 2021].

Taylor, M. (2019, March 11). Citizen Deliberation Is the Gateway to a Better Politics. *The Economist, Open Future*. [online]. Available at https://www.economist.com/open-future/2019/03/11/citizen-deliberation-is-the-gateway-to-a-better-politics [Last accessed 11 May 2021].

Thatcher, M. (1987, September 23). Interview for *Woman's Own* ("No Such Thing As Society") with Douglas Keay. Margaret Thatcher Foundation, Thatcher Archive (THCR 5/2/262): COI transcript. [online]. Available at https://www.margaretthatcher.org/document/106689 [Last accessed 11 May 2021].

Part three

A 'golden' path between the fiction, the framework, and real-world applications

25 Story as a strategy for sharing real world complex ideas

Great stories like *The Wonderful Wizard of Oz* capture our imagination because they speak to us on multiple levels. Baum's story entertains, but we also root for his characters because we identify with them, their struggles, and their desire to bring about change. If Baum intended his story to be an allegory, then there is meaning layered beyond even that, economic meaning that reveals his belief that monetary policy was the cause of inequality and injustice in his time – meaning which also pointed a path towards resolution.

Perhaps Baum's mastery of storytelling and the allegorical literary device he used was so great that it took us many years to uncover the story's alleged economic undertones. This deeper meaning was, reportedly, first identified by the historian Henry Littlefield in 1964.

Given that Baum's '*Wonderful Wizard of Oz*' was published in 1900, it means it took 64 years for this much-loved story's deeper meaning to surface. We can't wait that long to fix the dysfunctionality of today's economic system. Yes, we need stories that share complex ideas in an accessible way, so they stick and stay. But we need those stories that point to systemic solutions right away. We simply can't wait more than half a century to uncover embedded meaning – we need solutions now.

That's why we want to be transparent that the famous fictional fairy tale, which we've rewritten in the first part of this book, is an allegory for our times. We've also tried not to bury

DOI: 10.4324/9781003217657-29

that meaning too deep. It, we hope, paints a picture of a society worth fighting for, beyond the constraints of our current system. It points towards the circular economy as the pathway to lead us there. But, for the sake of absolute clarity, and to help directionally move us sooner rather than later towards a circular economy, here we offer the main themes we touch on in each of the fictional chapters and point to where we see they have crossover with the non-fiction aspects in part two of this book, with illustrative examples from our real world today.

References

Baum. (1900). *The Wonderful Wizard of Oz*. New York: George M. Hill Company.

Littlefield, H. (1964). The Wizard of Oz: Parable on Populism. *American Quarterly, 16*(1), 47–58. https://doi.org/10.2307/2710826.

26 Weathering extremities – real world themes

From this opening chapter, food and farming are recurrent themes. Dorie not only lives in a small farm-style house, as per Baum's original, but this is also now part of a working, albeit failing, dairy farm.

Fraught food

Since Baum's time of writing, we've experienced more than a century of commodification and consolidation in agriculture – impacting our land, food, and people. Dairy throughout is illustrative of the wider industrialised agriculture agenda and this chapter points to topics such as monocultures, pesticide usage, soil erosion, too much debt, overextended herd, milk gluts, price instability, and the imbalance of power within large scale, monopolistic supply chains.

- Nargi, L. (2018, November 05). What's Behind the Crippling Dairy Crisis? Family Farmers Speak Out. *Civil Eats*. [online]. Available at https://civileats.com/2018/11/05/whats-behind-the-crippling-dairy-crisis-family-farmers-speak-out/ [Last accessed 12 May 2021].

Flourishing food

Food is a reoccurring theme in the story because it is an excellent illustration of how both the productive and gatekept

DOI: 10.4324/9781003217657-30

economic cycles interplay. It is relatively easy to see how the four rules outlined in the productive cycle and summarised on **P90** could help transform our food system. But perhaps less obvious is how food's enclosure and its trade as a commodity, also sees it influenced by the gatekept cycle (also **P90**), raising questions around price stability, quality, and food security.

- Vivero, J. L. (2013, October 16). Why Food Should be a Commons Not a Commodity. *Our World, United Nations University*. [online]. Available at https://ourworld.unu.edu/en/why-food-should-be-a-commons-not-a-commodity [Last accessed 12 May 2021].

Extreme weather events

Today's economic system makes it profitable to pollute and poison our environment. A bleak picture of a dry and dusty Devon, and the tornado that follows, points to the link between the current take-make-dispose model in the productive economic cycle and climate change, which leads to the increased intensity and frequency of extreme weather events. In addition to deadly floods, bushfires, wildfires, sandstorms, record droughts, and rainfalls, disruptive weather patterns, like everything within an interconnected system, come full circle directly impacting water, food, and farming.

- Carbon Brief. (2021, February 25). Mapped: How Climate Change Affects Extreme Weather Around the World. *Carbon Brief: Clear on Climate*. [online]. Available at https://www.carbonbrief.org/mapped-how-climate-change-affects-extreme-weather-around-the-world [Last accessed 12 May 2021].
- Bosely, M. (2021, March 19). You Can't Escape the Smell: Mouse Plague Grows to Biblical Proportions Across Eastern Australia. *The Guardian*. [online]. Available at https://www.theguardian.com/australia-news/2021/

mar/19/you-cant-escape-the-smell-mouse-plague-grows-to-biblical-proportions-across-eastern-australia [Last accessed 12 May 2021].

- Greenpeace East Asia. (2021, March 19). Sandstorm Spreads Across East Asia, Bringing Orange Skies and Choking Air Pollution. [online Blog]. Available at https://webcache.googleusercontent.com/search?q=cache:pn8XP4Ldj-8J:https://www.greenpeace.org/eastasia/blog/6444/sandstorm-spreads-across-east-asia-bringing-orange-skies-and-choking-air-pollution/+&cd=1&hl=en&ct=clnk&gl=uk [Last accessed 12 May 2021].

27 From poor to paws – real world themes

Having awoken in Oz with Toto, Dorie meets the "People's Mayor" who tries to sell her on how great Oz is and to convince her to stay. Seeing it's a lost cause and that she won't get Dorie's vote, the People's Mayor quickly loses interest in her.

Servant leadership

This is the first direct reference in the story, again a recurring theme, to the role of democracy, our role within it, and why, for democracy to flourish, our elected government representatives must represent all people – not only themselves or those who vote for them.

In Abraham Lincoln's elegant words, at his Gettysburg Address in 1863, those elected to serve in democratic government are meant to be: 'Of the people, by the people, for the people'. It's a public service role, which to be representative requires an active, engaged, electorate. It points towards a fundamental question: Is our current economy democratic? Today's economy was built on a democratic social contract of mutuality. If widening inequality and injustice suggests our current economic model is in breach of contract, then let's renegotiate. Both the economy and democracy are living systems that can evolve and be reinvented. The interlinkages between democracy and the economy are further explored in the section: **A flourishing democracy is the path to a flourishing economy P165.**

DOI: 10.4324/9781003217657-31

Fast fashion

This chapter also returns to the imbalance of power within large scale, industrialised supply chains, this time in relation to what Dorie is wearing. Fast fashion does not feature within the second part of the book, but the circularity of materials, in this case textiles, is a critical aspect of the productive cycle, so the four rules summarised on **P90** would apply. This article is also a useful reference:

- Thomas, D. (2019, September 03). Fashionopolis: The Price of Fast Fashion and the Future of Clothes. *The New York Times*. [online]. Available at https://www.nytimes.com/2019/09/03/books/review/how-fast-fashion-is-destroying-the-planet.html [Last accessed 12 May 2021].

28 From straw for brains to wise owls – real world themes

Dorie meets a rather unusual looking scarecrow wearing an owl onesie – worn to scare off unnatural pests called 'land vultures' – vultures are reportedly wary of owls.

Common land

Land here introduces the wider theme of the commons, and how economic rents, derived from enclosure, rob everyone of benefiting from scarce, valuable communal assets. You'll find more on the detrimental impacts of this on the economy in: **The world's gifts and who benefits from them** on **P126**. **Building the commons and productive infrastructure at all scales** is also the fourth rule for the gatekept cycle on **P143**.

Land vultures

The made-up term 'land vultures' and the accompanying description of their behaviour, is used to make it easier to visualise what, in essence, is happening when land is enclosed. You'll find the fuller detail for how this works in the chapter **Uncovering the big players: active but hidden in plain sight** on **P120** – particularly the subsections on **Real estate and monopolies and The world's gifts and who benefits from them.**

DOI: 10.4324/9781003217657-32

Henry George

The chapter also points towards possible alternative outcomes from land's enclosure. The reference to a 'land value fee' relates to the section on **Henry George and his footnote in history** on **P127**. This article also offers a short overview of George's ideas:

- Neklason, A. (2019, April 15). The 140-Year-Old Dream of 'Government without Taxation'. *The Atlantic.* [online]. Available at https://www.theatlantic.com/national/archive/2019/04/henry-georges-single-tax-could-combat-inequality/587197/ [Last accessed 12 May 2021].

Compensation for enclosure

The concept of land value fees corresponds with rule two in the gatekept cycle – to shift taxes and fees on **P138**. Citizens become the beneficiaries of such enclosure fees via a basic dividend, as a "kind of financial compensation", which corresponds with the first rule in the gatekept cycle on **P135**.

Regenerative farming

Dorie and the scarecrow both live on farms – albeit vastly different. Their shared interest though leads to a tour, highlighting the benefits of mixed and regenerative farming methods. These regenerative methods lead to healthier soils, sequestered carbon, and multiple cashflows.

While food and agriculture are not mentioned in the second part of the book, what the scarecrow is describing here is how it's possible to secure circular food systems by applying rules 1, 2, and 4 set out within the chapter **The productive cycle: Four rules for materials to flow not fail our economy** on **P114**.

Strong soil

Strong soil is foundational to resilient food systems. When soil is weak, the forecast is bleak, yet many of today's industrialised farming practices deplete soil strength.

What's happening within strong soil, promoted by these regenerative farming methods, is circularity. There's a symbiotic relationship between what we see, like plants, crops, trees, and what we don't, like the fungus/mycelium embedded in the soil. Below the surface, tiny fungal threads interact with roots, helping the soil absorb water and exchange minerals for sugars via photosynthesis. That reciprocity impacts yields from a food and farming perspective, but it's also critical to freshwater availability and atmospheric carbon levels. Strong soil then is integral to the circularity of living systems at different scales. This podcast with Hunter Lovins, where she describes the need for a circular economy of the soil is well worth a listen. The work of Dr Walter Jehne is also worth checking out. Tracy Frisch's comprehensive interview with him offers a great starting point:

- Lovins, H. (2016, May 31). The Circular Economy of Soil. *The Circular Economy Show.* [online Podcast]. Available at https://the-circular-economy-podcast.simplecast.com/episodes/hunter-lovins-on-the-circular-economy-of-ba448ab9 [Last accessed 12 May 2021].
- Jehne, W. (2019) Supporting the Soil Carbon Sponge. *Eco Farming Daily: Grow Crops, Raise Livestock, Grow Your Farm.* Interview by T. Frisch. [online]. Available at https://www.ecofarmingdaily.com/supporting-the-soil-carbon-sponge/ [Last accessed 12 May 2021].

Tax triggers

Regenerative agriculture requires more people. That becomes more economically attractive, and therefore more likely, when taxes and fees shift away from people (and all renewable energy) as set out in the gatekept cycle's second rule on **P138**.

29 Heartless

If only AI had EI – real world themes

Baum's tin woodman is now a high tech, no emotion robot with artificial intelligence capabilities.

DemocraTECH

While this chapter discusses tech, the core theme is primarily about democracy. For it's not tech, still lacking an inbuilt heart, but the decisions humans take that will determine whether tech enables or disables our democratic freedoms. This links to the section **The liberation and terrors of directly connecting people, places, and things** on **P154.**

Being biomimetic

When Dorie finds the robot, it is disassembling earlier robotic models and separating their now redundant parts into different piles – ready for reuse. This is precisely the 'design for disassembly' concept pioneered by McDonough and Braungart (2002) in their seminal book *Cradle to Cradle*. It relates to the second rule to be biomimetic. You'll find information on all of this in the chapter **The productive cycle: Four rules for materials to flow not fail our economy** on **P114.**

DOI: 10.4324/9781003217657-33

Health check and tech

Within this chapter, there's reference to a "fellow self-learning Nexus" working with doctors to help diagnose cancer. This is not fictitious. It's based on IBM's Watson.

While you'll not find reference to Watson in part two, it's illustrative here to show how high tech is already transforming healthcare. The article below makes this point:

- Balasubramanian, S. (2021, January 23). How Technology Is Rapidly Changing Cancer Care. *Forbes Magazine.* [online]. Available at https://www.forbes.com/sites/saibala/2021/01/23/technology-is-rapidly-changing-cancer-care/?sh=7dab21ee5e9f [Last accessed 12 May 2021].

Workplace (r)evolution

"Doesn't everyone here hate you for taking their jobs?" Dorie asks the robot, to which it replies: "Quite the contrary. We exist to give humans the freedom to engage in more creative pursuits." There's no escaping that tech, as a critical element within our economy (established in the chapter **Worldview pre-science on P99),** is and will continue to transform the world of work. Yet, it's frequently reported as a given that tech is a threat to many livelihoods and ruinous to lives – with nothing we can do about it. It's ruinous to lives because good work matters beyond the income it provides. But that perilous prediction need not be a self-fulfilling prophecy. With the right proactivity, governance, and supporting mechanisms in place, like paying citizens a basic dividend, shifting taxes away from renewables (including human labour), and selling performance and service, tech could enable a positive shift in work. You'll find details of the first two supporting mechanisms in rules 1 and 2 in the chapter **The gatekept cycle: Four rules for money to circulate not clot our economy** from **P133.** The details for the third supporting mechanism is rule 3 in the chapter **The productive cycle: Four rules for materials to flow not fail our economy on P118.**

Reference

McDonough, W. and Braungart, M. (2002). *Cradle to Cradle. Remaking the Way We Make Things*. Berkeley, CA: North Point Press.

30 Making the lion's share enough to go around – real-world themes

Bryan the lion draws on his family heritage, his product, and his business model in this chapter to introduce Dorie to some key concepts. These include:

- The value of local community and how communities flourish. We discuss this in more detail in the chapter **A flourishing democracy is the path to a flourishing economy P165**.
- The importance of the flow of money; to be effective, it must work at different scales – explained further in the chapter **Shifting the metaphor: From machine to metabolism P105**.
- The benefit of a basic dividend for energising enterprise, which is the first rule in the chapter **The gatekept cycle: Four rules for money to circulate not clot our economy on P135**.

William Jennings Bryan

The story's fictional 'Bryan the lion' is a descendant of the late, real-world, American orator and presidential nominee, William Jennings Bryan. Bryan campaigned hard against tying the US currency to available gold supplies because it led to there being insufficient dollars available for exchange. This, Bryan argued, caused immense hardship, deflation, and benefitted only creditors.

DOI: 10.4324/9781003217657-34

Golden speech

Bryan made his case in dramatic fashion, in his most famous 'cross of gold' speech in 1896 (available online at https://en.wikipedia.org/wiki/Cross_of_Gold_speech). Within it, Bryan sets out the economy should not be nailed to the 'cross of gold'. Instead, silver, which was much more readily available, should additionally become part of the monetary base. Today, we have dispensed with any commodity tie-in.

Bryan influences Baum?

Bryan's 'cross of gold' speech happened only a few years before Baum published *The Wonderful Wizard of Oz*. It is this that many scholars (like Littlefield in 1964 in his *Parable on Populism*), believe Baum may have really been writing about and hid below the surface story.

Accessing assets

While President Nixon ("the Nixon shock") ended the link between America's monetary base and metals in 1971, it's a reminder that this was another twist on the assets versus commons power struggle. Bryan saw access to currency as a necessary public utility, and there are parallels we might again draw today as access to cash continues to become more difficult.

Cash crisis

This chapter offers the first mention in the story about the role cash plays within an economy. This goes on to become a central theme later in the story when the Great Wizard sets Dorie a challenge to look at the interplay between digital and physical money. While this interplay isn't a big focus within part two (see **P144**), cash and its circulation is critical to an inclusive economy. Offered here are some excellent reports and articles that highlight 'the magical disappearing act of cash' in real-world economies and some immediate implications:

- ACR. (2019). *The Access to Cash Review – Final Report, March 2019*. Chaired by N. Ceeney. Available at https://www.accesstocash.org.uk/media/1087/final-report-final-web.pdf [Last accessed 12 May 2021].
- Davidson, H. (2020, October 12). Chinese City Giving Away 10m Yuan in Lottery Trial of Digital Currency. *The Guardian*. [online]. Available at https://www.theguardian.com/world/2020/oct/12/chinese-city-giving-away-10m-yuan-in-lottery-trial-of-digital-currency [Last accessed 12 May 2021]
- Hearing, N. (2018, December 10). Who Is Behind the Campaign to Rid the World of Cash? *Real-World Economics Review, Issue 86*, 2–14. Available at http://www.paecon.net/PAEReview/issue86/Haering86.pdf [Last accessed 12 May 2021].
- Peachey, K. (2021, September 3). Coin Hoarding at Home Leads to Charity Plea. *BBC News*. [online]. Available at https://www.bbc.co.uk/news/business-58421192 [Last accessed 26 September 2021].

Community coinage

There are plenty of historical examples of local currencies. In this chapter, a fictional 'courageous community coin' has a value of '1sPence' stated on one side and a slogan on the other.

Thomas Spence

Coining the word '1sPence' is a nod to Thomas Spence (1750–1814). Spence, a very real-world early English radical, advocated for gender equality and capturing land value surplus. His vision was to use the economic rents from land at a parish level to benefit the whole community – including for women's education.

To advertise his ideas, Spence created tokens or over-stamped existing ones with political slogans. The slogan in the story: 'If you want apples you have to shake the tree' is a real-world proverb, but not one of Spence's slogans. It simply seemed fitting with the story given that it's embossed on tokens made from recycled cider bottle tops. For more on Spence, see:

- Thomas Spence Society. (2018). Thomas Spence. [online]. Available at http://www.thomas-spence-society.co.uk/ [Last accessed 12 May 2021].

Money at different scales

In Spence's time, Parliament deemed him politically radical, forbidding his organisation and censuring his ideas. Spence offers insight here, but the reference to him is primarily to illustrate that, as in the productive cycle, diversity is important, and money too has and can be done on different scales.

In this article, Gowen presents an overview of how a small Austrian town successfully experimented with its own local currency between 1932 and 1933.

- Gowen. (2021, January 17). Currency Solutions for a Wiser World – The Wörgl Experiment: Austria (1932–1933). *Lietaer*. [online]. Available at https://www.lietaer.com/2010/03/the-worgl-experiment/ [Last accessed 12 May 2021].

31 Locked in the past – real world themes

Dorie finally arrives at the Emerald City, ironically a gated community, with Baum's Guardian of the Gates reimagined as a grumpy gate greeter.

This scene led to the term 'the Gatekept cycle'. To understand the full meaning behind why we called it that, see the feature box on **P88.** Conceptually, this 'gatekept' term is interchangeable with what is often referred to as the 'Tollbooth economy'.

Access costs

This chapter's key theme is about how technology is transforming every sector. While that's exciting for many, not everyone welcomes that change and some, as the grumpy gate greeter, are excluded by it. The gate greeter's demeanour is a direct consequence of the loss of his business. It further illustrates an earlier point that work is about more than a wage, it's about a person's standing, their sense of worth, and the contribution they make within society.

When the gate greeter tells Dorie she must wear a smartwatch while in the Emerald City, this hints to the cost of entry to gated communities – whether the charge is immediately obvious (financial) or not (personal data). This is explored in the section **The liberation and terrors of making market access easier on P153** and also relates directly to the need for **rule 4 to build the commons on P143.**

DOI: 10.4324/9781003217657-35

Secret symbols

This is also the chapter where Dorie first sees the '**1. 2. 4 / 4**' symbol, set into the ironwork of the locked gates. This numerical device, more accurately described as a sigil in the second part of the book, is the unlock to the framework for economic change towards a circular economy. You'll find an overview of the framework and what each of the sigil's numbers represents on **P87.**

SPQR

The 'hidden in plain sight' symbol within the story, is from something in the real world, believed to date back as far as 80 B.C. It relates to "Senatus Populusque Romanus", often abbreviated to SPQR, which roughly translates as the 'Senate and the Roman people'. It's meant to signify Government and the people of the ancient Roman Republic working together because 'authority comes from the people'. You'll see it today inscribed on monuments and the municipality of Rome continues to use it as an official emblem. It's used in the story to signify the powerful interconnection between the economy and democracy.

32 Technological wizardry or trickery – real world themes

Dorie's arrival into the Emerald City doesn't go to plan when she's mugged for the smartwatch she's forced to wear while in the city. This incident raises questions in Dorie's mind about tech accessing personal data and how that can, or might in the future, be helpful or harmful to humans. This relates to the chapter **The liberation and terrors of a digital world on P150.** The following resources also offer illustrative insights:

- Parkins, K. (2021, February 26). OCT West Coast: How Can Decentralisation Help Optimise Rare Disease Trials? *Clinical Trials Arena*. [online]. Available at www.clinicaltrialsarena.com/analysis/rare-disease-research-decentralised-trials/ [Last accessed 12 May 2021].
- BBC TWO. (2016, December 07). Meet Emma: Parkinson's has Had a Devastating Impact on the Graphic Designer's Ability to Draw, But This Extraordinary Invention Could Help Change Her Life. *The Big Life Fix*. [online video clip]. Available at www.bbc.co.uk/programmes/p04jylxm [Last accessed 12 May 2021].
- Love, B. (2020, November 20). Covid Tracing Fans Public Health vs Privacy Debate. *Financial Times*. [online]. Available at https://www.ft.com/content/269d82ce-4523-4023-946f-9ded91ba63fc [Last accessed 12 May 2021].

DOI: 10.4324/9781003217657-36

Cash or cashless challenge

Dorie also has her first, virtual, interaction with the Great Wizard of Oz in this chapter. It is during this initial encounter that the Great Wizard agrees to get Dorie home in exchange for her doing something in return. Not, as Baum tasks Dorothy to do and kill the Wicked Witch of the West, but something, to Dorie, that seems equally out of her comfort zone and daunting: to advise the Wizard on whether Oz should become a cashless society. You'll find the details on this in the **Cash Crisis section on P189.** Dorie's reticence to undertake the Wizard's challenge also links to the theme of democracy and the importance of citizens playing an active role in it, which you'll find in more detail in the chapter: **A flourishing democracy – the path to a flourishing economy on P165**.

33 The wonderful Emerald City – real world themes

Dorie tours the Emerald City, which sees her discover key circularity design themes.

Waste=food

The reference to how the great city feeds itself (biological sphere), and the reference to product passports (technical sphere), both relate to the waste=food concept. That's where the waste of one domain becomes food for another.

Waste=food relates to the second change principle – to be biomimetic. You'll find details related to this in the chapter about **The productive cycle: Four rules for materials to flow not fail our economy** on **P114**.

Product passports

Product passports are about how tech is enabling supply chain transparency – a critical element to materials circularity. To find out more about this passport concept, the start-up 'Circularise' in the Netherlands is an illustrative example.

- Circularise. (n.d.). Disrupting Long-Held Linear Systems. *Circularise*. Available at https://www.circularise.com/about. [Last accessed 12 May 2021].

DOI: 10.4324/9781003217657-37

Fractal cities

The reference to the City's design, which is described as 'clusters of interconnected mazes' is in direct reference to fractal cities. This paper offers an introduction:

- Salingaros, N. A. (2004). *Connecting the Fractal City*. Keynote speech at the 5th Biennial of Towns and Town Planners in Europe (Barcelona, April 2003). First published in PLANUM: *The European Journal of Planning*, March 2004. [online]. Available at https://applied.math.utsa.edu/~yxk833/connecting.html [Last accessed 12 May 2021].

Coffee, cash, & computer chips

The seemingly mundane activity to grab a coffee gives Dorie reason to think about the challenge she's been set by the Great Wizard and the role cash plays within society. You'll find the details on this in the **Cash Crisis section on P189.**

Pocket change

Before even entering the coffee shop, Dorie's encounter with a homeless girl reminds her of a poster 'keep your coins, I want change'. The inspiration here is from a real world, rumoured Banksy piece, in Melbourne. The implied deeper meaning being that the person depicted is asking for social change, not loose pocket change.

- Canvas Art Rocks. (2021, May 07). UPDATED 2021! 136 Amazing Banksy Graffiti Artworks with Locations. [online blog]. Available at https://us.canvasartrocks.com/blogs/posts/70529347-121-amazing-banksy-graffiti-artworks-with-locations [Last accessed 12 May 2021].

Oz-nomic policies

Dorie also learns in this chapter about some more economic policies the Wizard has used to enable the city and its people to sparkle. These directly correspond to some of the key principles in part two as outlined below.

When medic Matt explains to Dorie that he rents not owns his apartment he says: "We had to make a choice. It came down to ownership or affordable access. It started with housing, but it goes way beyond that now – this city is built on a service model." This corresponds with rule 2 to **shift taxes and fees towards non-renewables** on **P138** and rule 3 to **shift from selling goods to services and performance** on **P118**.

Later in the chapter, medic Matt says: "The Wizard's vision is all about giving people access to Oz's communal assets and resources to be productive." This relates to rule 4 to **build the commons and productive infrastructure at all scales** outlined on **P143**.

The upshot of Dorie's tour is ultimately that while the Emerald City is wonderful, it isn't perfect.

34 The magical festival of urban food – real world themes

It's at this festival that Dorie has her ideas challenged about industrialised food systems.

Community cuisine

While helping prepare food at the festival, the first thing Dorie learns about is community cuisine. These community style cooking and dining experiences are very real and increasingly popular. You can find out more about community kitchens in these resources:

- Big Bold Cities. (2018). Mexico City Community Kitchens: A Community Solution for Food Insecurity. *Big Bold Cities: Democratic Innovation in World Cities*. [online]. Available at https://bigboldcities.org/en/innovation/community-kitchens [Last accessed 12 May 2021].
- Shareable. (2013). *Sharing Cities: Activating the Urban Commons*. San Francisco, CA: Tides Center/Shareable.
- Bentley, S. (2017, May 19). Why the World Needs Community Kitchens. *TEDx Talk*. [online]. Available at https://www.youtube.com/watch?v=g7ab3eN9qPo [Last accessed 12 May 2021].

DOI: 10.4324/9781003217657-38

Global and local food

Dorie learns that Oz has moved away from the tired 'global versus local' debate by embracing all operational scales – effectively speaking to another core circularity principle: To celebrate diversity and optimise the whole system (rule 4) contained in the chapter **The productive cycle: Four rules for materials to flow not fail our economy** on **P114.**

These articles demonstrate some emerging high tech, low carbon initiatives that illustrate global and local food systems working in tandem in the real world:

- Vegconomist. (2020, December 03). Finland: Protein from Thin Air by Solar Foods Get Commercial Go-Ahead. *Vegconomist: The Vegan Business Magazine*. [online]. Available at https://vegconomist.com/science/finland-protein-from-thin-air-by-solar-foods-gets-commercial-go-ahead/ [Last accessed 12 May 2021].
- Dyson, L. (2016, July 24). A Forgotten Space Age Technology Could Change How We Grow Food. *TED Talks*. [online]. Available at https://www.youtube.com/watch?v=c8WMM_PUOjo [Last accessed 12 May 2021].

Platforms for produce

When the sack truck guy speaks to Dorie while delivering his produce, he talks about making use of platform technology to design out waste from the food system. This links to the section **The liberation and terrors of directly connecting people, places, and things P154** – particularly the example of *FareShare Go* in the UK.

Fake steak

The inspiration for the 'bleeding' fake steak that Dorie digs into at dinner is based on the Beyond Burger by the *Beyond Meat* company.

- Young, S. (2018, November 12). 'Bleeding' Vegan Burger Launches in Tesco Stores Across the UK. *The Independent.* [online]. Available at https://www.independent.co.uk/life-style/bleeding-vegan-burger-beyond-meat-tesco-uk-supermarket-health-plant-based-a8629431.html [Last accessed 12 May 2021].

Table talk – money and politics

Dorie's dinner table conversation extends beyond food to other circularity themes. She gains an understanding of the roles of a basic dividend, explained on **P135**.

Dorie also wonders 'who decides how much basic dividend is enough?' That question links to the chapter **A flourishing democracy is the path to a flourishing economy** on **P165**.

The 'magic cakes' are simply used as another illustrative way to return to the theme about the role cash plays within an economy – as discussed in the **Cash Crisis** section on **P189.**

35 The nightmare of Oz the Terrible – real world themes

In a dream, Dorie meets her equivalent of Baum's Wicked Witch of the West – Oz the Terrible. Having fallen foul of the laws of the land, Dorie finds herself in a grand court room answering to Oz the Terrible who has accumulated masses of digital data on her. This Terrible Oz is judge, jury, and displeased.

This entire chapter, about tech's shadow side, relates to **The liberation and terrors of directly connecting people, places, and things** on **P154**.

Sesame and social credit systems

This chapter includes a fictionalisation of real-world social and sesame credit systems to illustrate how digital data can begin to converge to build a powerful picture of a person.

The social credit system emerging in China is a complex system where unique identity codes link individuals and businesses to a permanent digital record. Today, China's system is regionally varied, but it's fictionalised in the story to illustrate how multiple digital technologies can converge and might, in the wrong hands, become Big Brotherish in style, to restrict democratic freedoms. Indeed, some reports (including the one mentioned below by Nicole Kobie), already indicate that there's a 'blacklist' linked to this social credit system – so 'if you owe the government money, you could lose certain rights'. Imagine if

DOI: 10.4324/9781003217657-39

all an economy's money were to become digital. As a purely digital technology, money would become linkable to such a system. Getting blacklisted and losing certain rights, while extreme, could include suspending someone's ability to pay.

This, then, uncovers a tension between the benefits of a basic dividend, paid to citizens in digital currency into a central bank account, and a potential threat to autonomy. In the digital world, it is easy to get all sorts of seemingly unrelated things to talk to each other. In an 'internet of things', digital money simply becomes another 'thing' that could/would connect. That's why, while not necessarily obvious today, when the possibility exists for a remote third party to instantly 'switch off' an individual's choices, the disappearance of cash from society is a real threat to autonomy. Diversity brings strength; digital and physical money are both needed within the economy because cash represents freedom. It's yet further evidence of the intrinsic link between our economy and democracy.

You'll find information relating to:

- central bank accounts on **P208**
- paying a basic dividend on **P135**
- the disappearance of cash from the economy in **Cash Crisis** on **P189**
- the interplay between our economy and democracy on **P165**

These resources may also be of interest:

- Kobie, N. (2019, June 07). The Complicated Truth about China's Social Credit System. *Wired*. [online]. Available at https://www.wired.co.uk/article/china-social-credit-system-explained [Last accessed 12 May 2021].
- Mosher, S. W. (2019, May 18). China's New 'Social Credit System' is a Dystopian Nightmare. *New York Post*. [online]. Available at https://nypost.com/2019/05/18/chinas-new-social-credit-system-turns-orwells-1984-into-reality/ [Last accessed 12 May 2021].

- Zuboff, S. (2021, February 19). *How Surveillance Capitalism Is Undermining Democracy*. Interview by Hari Sreenivasan PBS. [online video and transcript]. Available at https://www.pbs.org/wnet/amanpour-and-company/video/how-surveillance-capitalism-is-undermining-democracy/ [Last accessed 12 May 2021].

36 Meeting the wonderful Wizard of Oz – real world themes

Cash challenge

When meeting the wonderful Wizard of Oz, Dorie offers her thoughts on the cash challenge. She advocates for the importance of keeping cash and highlights why phasing it out would be a profound mistake. With the economy and democracy interwoven, the removal of cash is more than an economic decision – it's a democratic one. This relates to the chapter **A flourishing democracy – the path to a flourishing economy** on **P165.** You'll find all the additional resources in the **Cash Crisis** section on **P189.**

Costly cash

Dorie's acknowledgement that "cash costs" speaks to rule 4 to **optimise the whole system** on **P118**. An efficient part (cash) will never be enough – a diverse and effective whole monetary system is what's required to secure resilience. There's a delicate yet necessary balance to strike between efficiency and resilience, which relates to the section **What makes an effective system?** referencing Sally Goerner's work on **P109.**

Creating money

"It's within my gift to determine who creates the money," the Wizard explains to Dorie. How and where money is created

DOI: 10.4324/9781003217657-40

need not be fixed and this is explored in the chapter **Finance: A big active player hidden in plain sight**, specifically the sub-sections that reference Mary Mellor's Magic money trees on **P124**.

"When I took charge of this beautiful land, I was told I couldn't spend more than I raised from taxes or borrowed," the Wizard tells Dorie. The Wizard's words here mirror the narrative about our own real-world economy: You can only spend what you first raise. But that's not true. That thinking is, as the Wizard explains to Dorie, "back to front". If Government really could 'only spend what it first raises', it would not have been possible for Governments, in Britain in particular, to spend as they have during the pandemic.

Pandemic spending is evidence that any Government, with its own stable currency, can "spend money into existence that's needed first and tax it back afterwards", and there doesn't need to be a pandemic to do it – they can do it any time.

But what about our having to pay back all that additional spend and the severe austerity measures that must surely follow because of that mounting debt and deficit? Also a fiction. What usually happens after a big Government splurge is people and public services are punished with high taxes, austerity measures and selling off 'common wealth' to 'balance the books'.

- Inman, P. (2021, March 27). Britain's Public Wealth and Health Are Up for Sale Again. *The Guardian*. [online]. Available at https://www.theguardian.com/business/2021/mar/27/britains-public-wealth-and-health-are-up-for-sale-again [Last accessed 12 May 2021].

That reaction by Government leads most of us to believe that a Country's deficit is something bad, to be avoided at all costs. But as Stephanie Kelton lays bare in her aptly titled book 'The Deficit Myth' the narrative that Government borrowing is bad is flawed. Deficits, when the money is used productively (within the Productive cycle), can strengthen and build a better economy.

This 'deficit is doom' myth is reinforced not because the Government borrows or creates new money, but because of where the money is incentivised to be spent (often unproductively in assets that extract wealth – the gatekept cycle), and how Government behaves afterwards to claw all the money back to "rebalance" (often from the Productive cycle where money fulfils its intended purpose – to circulate and work hard).

Low, zero, or negative real interest rates mean it doesn't cost Government (with a sovereign currency) much or anything to borrow, neither does Government have to pay everything it borrows back – it can issue more bonds at the due date. The Government is just like a bank. The public sector's deficit is the private sector's surplus. Governments can spend money into existence first, get it into people's hands, and put it to good use. They can incentivise its spend within the economy's Productive cycle and disincentivise spend on wealth-extracting assets in its Gatekept cycle. Two chapters in part two explain why the Productive cycle is critical to a circular economy and how we could start to shift spending towards it.

- The Productive cycle on **P114**
- The Gatekept cycle on **P133**

Pandemic spending, at least in the UK, has seen Government create and borrow money and broadly put it 'to good use' in the Productive cycle. It places us at a tipping point, there is a genuine opportunity to #BuildBackBetter. Whether we realise this opportunity or not will be determined by what happens next. A reaction that leads to the punishment of the Productive cycle – squeezing wages, damaging public services, or generally taxing productivity, isn't the only response.

"1% NHS pay rise is 'the most we can afford' for nurses," said the UK's Health Minister in March 2021. This is an illustrative example, but it needn't be the default, tired, untrue narrative from Government in building a post-pandemic economy. There are other options that enable us to #BuildBackBetter. As citizens in a democracy, we can actively engage with Government and challenge what happens next to change the economic narrative.

"The moment it stops being permissible to question the fundamental assumptions of an economic system that is patently dysfunctional is the moment political freedom ends and cultural repression begins," Tim Jackson beautifully articulates in the prologue to the second edition of his book '*Prosperity Without Growth*' (Abingdon, Oxon: Routledge). This is a book that morphed to unexpected international success from a UK Sustainable Development Commission report, exploring the relationship between prosperity and sustainability. Reportedly deemed ill-timed and ill-titled for the then UK Government (launched the week of the G20 in London in 2009 to 'kick-start growth' following the 2008 financial crash), the report (and its ideas, some of which are echoed in this book), was effectively "buried". Today, more than a decade later, we still have that very same "patently dysfunctional economic system". Yet, now we find ourselves in a different time, with a different Government, and with a different mindset – with recent citizen activism suggesting a greater willingness to get our collective voice heard.

In Baum's original story, Dorothy discovers her silver slippers have the power to take her home. They've been on her feet from the outset of her journey in Oz. Dorothy has always had the power. While we might not realise it, Governments too 'have the power'. The power to create money, the power to bring about spend in the Productive cycle, the power to print or borrow money to solve all kinds of societal problems, including, for example, investments towards tackling climate change. But we too 'have the power' to 'lobby government' and bring about the systemic economic change we need and seek.

Central bank accounts

In the secret room accessed from her office, the Wizard reveals a data storage centre to Dorie. The Wizard tells Dorie: "These servers hold a central bank account for everyone in Oz – their basic dividend gets paid into it." In development today are central bank digital currencies, which offer an opportunity to make payments directly to citizens. See for instance:

- Wikipedia. (2021, May 07). Central Bank Digital Currency. *Wikipedia the Free Encyclopaedia*. [online]. Available at https://en.wikipedia.org/wiki/Central_bank_digital_currency [Last accessed 12 May 2021].

Metronome synchronization

Before going their separate ways, the Wizard reveals a critical truth to Dorie. With one simple adjustment, the Wizard synchronises some metronomes. The Wizard is demonstrating to Dorie that you don't have to change everything when things are out of order or incoherent to get a different, more harmonious, result – it's about synchronising systems, 'entraining' them. You can see this Synchronization of Metronomes experiment being demonstrated by Harvard Natural Sciences here:

- Harvard Natural Sciences. (2010, June 08). Synchronization of Metronomes Experiment. *Harvard Natural Sciences Lecture Demonstrations*. [online YouTube clip]. Available at https://www.youtube.com/watch?v=Aaxw4zbULMs [Last accessed 12 May 2021]. Reproduced from B. Daniels. (2005), Synchronization of Globally Coupled Nonlinear Oscillators: The Rich Behavior of the Kuramoto Model. [online]. Available at http://go.owu.edu/~physics/StudentResearch/2005/BryanDaniels/index.html [Last accessed 12 May 2021].

37 Back home and Chasing rainbows – real world themes

In a departure from Baum's original ending, Dorie doesn't neatly land back home to live happily ever after.

The somewhat dogeared Wonderful Circles of Oz document (due to its constant review and adjustment over decades), designed to help Dorie bring about real-world economic change, is a reminder that change is both constant and difficult.

No matter how good an economic model and how great our resulting lives become, we simply don't live in a perfect world. There will always be tensions to resolve because progress is iterative and there is no year zero. What we have to secure the economy and the ending we both want and need, is ourselves. What we do in the here and now will determine our future. These final two chapters then directly correlate with active participation in democracy and the chapter **A flourishing democracy – the path to a flourishing economy** on **P165.**

DOI: 10.4324/9781003217657-41

Afterword from the authors

This book has been five years in the making and as we come to write these final words, COVID-19 continues to wrong-foot the world as we know it. As this invisible virus continues to mutate and spread through the planet, if ever there were evidence that we are part of an interdependent and circulatory ecosystem, this is it.

And, while the virus itself is indiscriminate, the economic impact it is wreaking is not. Work and income are again at the fore. Early in the pandemic, The International Labour Organisation suggested that "almost half the global workforce 1.6 billion people are in immediate danger of having their livelihoods destroyed" (Inman, 2020). Two years on and the economic impacts are still being acutely felt globally yet disproportionately. Food security is but one of COVID's devastating impacts on livelihoods and futures, with the World Food Programme estimating 111 million more people are without sufficient food in the 35 countries it works (The World Bank, 2021).

Inequality and precarious work is widening and starkly revealing just how far we have diverged from a social contract based in democracy. From the side-lines, most (at least in the most unequal 'democracies' like the UK and USA) are watching in disbelief as centralised political personalities battle between keeping people alive or keeping the economy alive.

In Baum's original story, it is Dorothy's dog, Toto, who knocks over a screen to reveal the Great Wizard is not so great. It seems an animal (likely a bat or bird) may again be a catalyst – this time for COVID-19 – which is once more exposing a hugely disappointing truth. It lays bare, not only the fragility of our interconnected planet that we all call home, but it raises critical questions in the minds of billions – about democracy, about politics and about what our economy is for and who it serves.

In her book the *Shock Doctrine*, Naomi Klein (2008) argues that it is possible to change the status quo following a shocking national or pan-national event. A global pandemic that kills millions, closes borders, pauses capitalism, and halts the world – it is hard to imagine anything more shocking than this.

Yet, as Klein herself shows in her book, it is economic stories that determine how the status quo is altered – something Black Death historian, Walter Scheidel, agrees with:

> What I'm very sceptical about is the idea that ideology, or rhetoric, or just political agitation by itself can change things. What you need is essentially a combination of certain kind of ideas being out there, and then a shock to the established order that allows those ideas to become mainstream.
>
> (Scheidel, 2008)

Now is the time for a new economic story. Not one penned by a phoney Wizard in some far away glitzy city who we believe magically holds all the answers but by us – rewriting our economic story until it becomes one we can identify with. For the moral of Baum's classic story is surely that four, ordinary, underconfident, characters embark on a difficult journey only to discover that they always held all the answers they seek when they are brave enough to look within.

Robert J. Shiller has demonstrated, economic narratives are no different to other stories. Those we re-tell are those that resonate and those that resonate, spread. Stories are powerful. They can be as contagious as any virus, infecting those they touch as they spread.

> Disease epidemiology has shown us that there will likely be repeats of variants of older epidemics in the future as reservoirs

> of old epidemics mutate or react to a changed environment to start a new wave of contagion. There will be new forms of influenza and new influenza epidemics. So, too, many [old economic] narratives... will become epidemic again, weaken after years have passed, and then rise once more... Powerful economic narratives of the past that are mostly inactive and sometimes largely forgotten... are not completely forgotten, and someone seeking a powerful story may rediscover them.
> (Shiller, 2019, p. 271)

We already have all the elements to create a great new economic story enabling us to #BuildBackBetter, one that combines certain kinds of long forgotten ideas and reimagines them in a fresh new way – a fully circular way. One that casts us as the main protagonist. And, one that has a happy ending because it works for us – wherever we live and call home.

All we need to do now is start telling it.

We sign off with this, taken from the story that inspired this book, the original 'Wonderful Wizard of Oz' (Baum, 1990).

"My darling child!" cried Aunt Em, folding the little girl in her arms and covering her face with kisses. "Where in the world did you come from?"

"From the Land of Oz' said Dorothy gravely. 'And here is Toto, too. And oh, Aunt Em! I'm so glad to be at home again!"

With heartfelt thanks to L. Frank Baum. Whether rooted in fact or fiction his beautifully crafted story 'The Wonderful Wizard of Oz' has inspired generations of children... and adults.

References

Baum. (1900). *The Wonderful Wizard of Oz*. New York: George M. Hill Company.

Inman, P. (2020, April 29). Half of the World's Workers at Immediate Risk of Losing Livelihood Due to Coronavirus. *The Guardian* [online]. Available at https://www.theguardian.com/world/2020/apr/29/half-of-worlds-workers-at-immediate-risk-of-losing-livelihood-due-to-coronavirus [Last accessed 12 May 2021].

Klein, N. (2008). *The Shock Doctrine: The Rise of Disaster Capitalism*. London: Penguin.

Scheidel, W. (2020, April 30). Black Death Historian: A Coronavirus Depression Could be a Great Leveller. Interviewed by Kyrill Hartog. *The Guardian*. [online]. Available at https://www.theguardian.com/world/commentisfree/2020/apr/30/walter-scheidel-a-shock-to-the-established-order-can-deliver-change [Last accessed 12 May 2021].

Shiller, R. J. (2019). *Narrative Economics: How Stories Go Viral and Drive Major Economic Events*. Princeton, NJ: Princeton University Press.

The World Bank. (2021, May 07). Food Security and COVID-19. [online]. Available at https://www.worldbank.org/en/topic/agriculture/brief/food-security-and-covid-19 [Last accessed 12 May 2021].